What Time Is This Place?

Kevin Lynch

The MIT Press Cambridge, Massachusetts and London, England

Copyright © 1972 by
The Massachusetts Institute of Technology

This book was designed by Kevin Lynch and
produced by the MIT Press Media Department.
It was set in Linofilm Palatino
by Southern New England Typographic Service,
printed on Finch Filmtext
by The Colonial Press, Inc.
and bound in Interlaken AV1 428
by The Colonial Press, Inc.
in the United States of America.

Library of Congress Cataloging in Publication Data

Lynch, Kevin.
    What time is this place?

    Bibliography: p.
    1. Progress—Addresses, essays, lectures. 2. Cycles—Ad-
dresses, essays, lectures. 3. Time perception—Addresses, essays, lectures. I. Title.
CB155.L95   301.24   72–7059
ISBN 0–262–12061–5

I have seen land made from the sea; and far away from the ocean the sea-shells lay, and old anchors were found there on the tops of mountains. That which was a plain, a current of water has made into a valley, and by a flood the mountain has been levelled into a plain. The ground that was swampy is parched with dry sand, and places which have endured drought are wet with standing pools. The heavens, and whatever there is beneath them, and the earth, and whatever is upon it, change their form.

Ovid, *Metamorphoses*, Book XV

To:
Howard Webber
Michael Southworth
Mary Potter
Catherine Lynch
Anne Lynch
Karalyn Krasin
Gyorgy Kepes,

whose ideas helped me write this book.

Contents

List of Illustrations

What Time Is This Place?

Introduction: Time and Place

Change and recurrence are the sense of being alive—things gone by, death to come, and present awareness. The world around us, so much of it our own creation, shifts continually and often bewilders us. We reach out to that world to preserve or to change it and so to make visible our desire. The arguments of planning all come down to the management of change.

This book deals with the evidence of time which is embodied in the physical world, how those external signals fit (or fail to fit) our internal experience, and how that inside-to-outside relationship might become a life-enhancing one. The discussion ranges from historical preservation to the forms of transition, futurism, time signals, the esthetics of time, biological rhythm, time perception, disaster, renewal, and revolution.

The theme of the book is that the quality of the personal image of time is crucial for individual well-being and also for our success in managing environmental change, and that the external physical environment plays a role in building and supporting that image of time. The relationship is therefore reciprocal.

I shall argue that a desirable image is one that celebrates and enlarges the present while making connections with past and future. The image must be flexible, consonant with external reality, and, above all, in tune with our own biological nature. What these generalities signify will appear later. Throughout the discussion the reader will find a strong emphasis on the present—where we are and must live—and on the necessity and desirability of change. This will at times be disturbing.

The book begins by sketching out several real cases of environmental change. Next there is a discussion of place as an emblem of past, present, and future time. These ideas are then knitted together with a synopsis of the biology, psychology, and sociology of time. One chapter illustrates the symbols of time in a particular place in order to convey a sense of what this specific time-place means to its residents. There follows an analysis of the esthetics of environmental time, a discussion of the crucial issues of environmental change management, and some thoughts on the relation (or lack of relation) between environmental and social change. A final chapter summarizes the ideas for policy which emerge from these discussions.

Cities Transforming

1

Environments change. A sudden disaster may destroy a city, farms will be made from wilderness, a loved place is abandoned, or a new settlement is built on an obscure frontier. Slower natural processes may transform an ancient landscape, or social shifts cause bizarre dislocations. In the midst of these events, people remember the past and imagine the future.

Instances of environmental transformation are common. On the one hand, people must endure them, and we see their efforts to preserve, create, or destroy the past, to make sense out of a rapid transition, or to build a secure sense of the future. On the other hand, the initiators and regulators of change—the developers, princes, planners, entrepreneurs, housebuilders, managers, public officials—struggle with these transformations in another way, straining to comprehend and control them. By citing a number of these cases, whose contrasts may be sharpened by the diversity of culture, place, and time, I mean to show that underneath this diversity there are some common themes for both initiator and endurer.

The fire began early Sunday morning, September 2, at a baker's house on Pudding Lane, in a city just recovering from the plague. Under an east wind the crowded medieval town burned out of control until Thursday morning. Indeed, cellars were still burning in the spring of 1667. Four-fifths of Europe's third-richest city lay in ashes, with 13,200 houses destroyed, 80,000 persons homeless, the damage near £10 million. The nation was at war with France and Holland, and its finances were strained. The coming winter proved especially severe, and the coal ships from Newcastle were frequently captured by Dutch privateers. Skilled labor, timber, brick, and stone were all in short supply.

For one hundred years the City of London had been growing rapidly but was beginning to lose population and trade to the surrounding suburbs. For the previous ten years the city's financial position had been declining. There were no maps, few accu-

London, 1666:
The Great Fire

Reference 88

rate title deeds, no long-term credits, no insurance. Properties were held under a complicated system of freeholds, leases, and subleases, with many intermixed ownerships. Widows, dependents, and charities relied on property income for their support. The legislation and administration to manage a vast rebuilding program did not exist.

But there were accepted political authorities and the will to recover. In the days immediately following the fire, royal and city proclamations set recovery in motion—clearing the streets, establishing watches, relocating administrative offices, requiring neighboring towns to open their gates to refugees, providing food and coal. On September 13 an interim royal proclamation declared that the new city would be built of brick and stone, that its streets would be widened, and that it would have a fine new riverfront. The hearth tax was lifted, the ruins were to be surveyed, and no rebuilding would be allowed that was not according to plan.

New standard street widths were set in October, and streets were cleared of rubbish by December. In February, Parliament passed a Rebuilding Act that set the guidelines for reconstruction and its financing. Detailed street plans were enacted by April. London would arise on its old ground plan but with widened streets, standard fireproof buildings, better utilities, and new markets. There were strong pressures to rebuild quickly. A long delay might cause dispossessed merchants to abandon the City permanently. Some had already left for other market towns. Most refugees first camped in the open spaces north of the City but soon found cramped lodgings in the unburned suburbs and surrounding towns or built temporary sheds in the ruins or under the walls. Orphans were sent to the country.

There was little building activity in 1667. Sites had to be cleared and surveyed, legal disputes untangled, and capital, labor, brick, and timber mobilized. Rents in the unburned areas rose steeply, even to three or four times their former levels. Site values in the burned areas fell. But a simple procedure for marking out the new streets and recovering the old building sites was established. A special Fire Court was set up to cut through legal mazes and to get property into the hands of owners or tenants able and willing to rebuild. Fragments of land on which building was impossible could be transferred, and sites on which owners refused to build could be acquired by compulsory purchase and resold. Official surveyors regulated property lines and the quality of construction. All buildings would now be built with brick or stone walls and according to one of three standard designs, which prescribed elevations, sections, materials, and construction details. Necessary timber supplies were easily expanded by importation from Scandinavia, but a network of brickyards had to be established about London, and supplies of stone remained chronically short. Public rebuilding was notably delayed by this shortage. Labor difficulties were solved by opening the city guilds to country craftsmen, over the protests of the London companies and journeymen. Provincial carpenters and bricklayers streamed in, attracted by steady work and high London wages. Wage levels were maintained, but craft divisions collapsed, and later on there was unemployment. The established road and water communications allowed labor and materials to reach the stricken city, and dependents and the homeless to be dispersed.

General building activity began in the spring of 1668, and by the end of that summer there were seven or eight hundred houses ready to be used principally as inns for the construction workers. Meanwhile, the ruins were at night the realm of criminals or the poor who had built their sheds there. By early 1669, John Evelyn could say that the City "began a little to revive," but one-third of the foundations had yet to be cleared and staked out, no churches had been rebuilt, few streets were paved. Most of the physical reconstruction occurred in 1669 and 1670 and was nearly finished by 1672. Public buildings and guildhalls were largely complete by then, markets and transport reestablished, and all but 960 of the eventual 8200 new houses were up.

But now the City learned that over 40 percent of those newly built houses were standing vacant, and one-quarter of the dispossessed population had not yet returned. Merchants and tradesmen had found it to their advantage to settle permanently in the suburbs, free from the restrictions and taxes of the guild city, continuing a move that had been going on since Elizabeth's reign. And the poor, once housed in the crowded cellars and wooden tenements of the city center, could not now afford the new brick houses. Rebuilding had pushed them out to the unregulated cottage districts on the fringe.

The City rejoiced in the latter move but saw in the former a serious blow to its power and wealth. It responded, not by attempting to extend its jurisdiction over the suburbs, but by trying to force those who traded in the city to live there and by futile measures to stop suburban building, one more of a long series of rulings that had been made since 1580.

The City debt had begun to rise in 1658 before the fire, and there were no public revenues or credits equal to the demands of the rebuilding task. In the emergency Parliament authorized a one-shilling (later a three-shilling) tax on each ton of imported coal, and it was this income that paid the public cost of reconstructing London. The coal tax was paid by Londoners. Moreover, it was local capital that rebuilt the shops and houses. Labor and materials were drawn from long distances, but the cash was London cash.

Of the £675,000 raised by the coal dues over twenty years, over half was spent on St. Paul's and the parish churches. The latter may in fact have been overbuilt, given the population they eventually served. Of the remainder of the coal dues, approximately one-quarter was spent on land for widened streets and new marketplaces; an eighth on paving, sewers, laystalls, wharves, stairs, and markets; an eighth on the new guildhall; a quarter for other public, nonreligious buildings (prisons, offices, trading halls); and a final quarter for the new Fleet Canal. The canal was an engineering success but a financial failure and was arched over in 1733 to make a road. Private rebuilding must have come to at least £3 million, or perhaps five times the public share, and there were substantial investments in guildhalls, the Royal Exchange, and various other institutions.

The City came close to bankruptcy in 1672 but

averted it by borrowing on the coal dues. In 1683, London was forced to declare a moratorium on the payment of its debts, and lost many of its privileges as a result. Most of the guilds were in financial difficulties until the 1740s. The London region continued to prosper, but the power of old London collapsed. The financial strain of rebuilding aggravated the historic failure to adapt to a new economy and a new spatial and social organization.

The new London, however, was a substantial improvement over the old. Commissioners took over the unified management of paving, leveling, draining, and clearing. Streets were widened to standard widths according to a rational hierarchy, bottlenecks were broken, and frontage lines were regularized. The narrowest lanes were set at 14 feet, wide enough for two drays to pass, and the widest major streets at 45 to 50 feet. Two continuous east-west routes that ran across the city were put together, and the approaches to the waterside, particularly to London Bridge, were opened up. The rubble of the ruins was used to level up the streets and to ease their gradients. Streets were paved and drained, and a protected way was provided for pedestrians. Markets were removed from the streets to new public areas. Public laystalls where waste could be collected and transferred to river barges were established. Public water outlets were moved out of the line of traffic. Offensive trades were segregated or displaced. The Exchange and the crossing of new routes created the first concentrated financial district.

Within the limits of contemporary financial and institutional ability, the new London was a successful response to the old problems of the medieval town. Large schemes, such as the Fleet Canal or the Thames Quay, failed in their aim. The former was built but little used. The latter was proposed but never carried through owing to lack of funds for embankment and of power to enforce the clearance of private land. (But the building line restrictions along that unborn quay survived for 150 years!) Despite these more spectacular failures, the replanned public services and the regulation of rebuilding were both highly effective. The new city did not adjust as well to its new economy, the changes in its population, or the shift from river traffic to road traffic. In these areas the City was planning for obsolete needs, but indeed most plans are preoccupied with the past. Moreover, and this is also not unusual, the changes bore most heavily on the poor.

The standardization of building design, the Fire Court, the street replanning, the methods for staking out, and the measures for increasing the supply of timber, brick, and labor were efficient actions for restoring and improving the City. The will to rebuild was strong, and much that was done to restore and improve the City was accomplished with efficiency and ingenuity. Barriers to action were unlocked by reducing uncertainties, by settling disputes rapidly, by making simple public directives and seeing that information was easily accessible. As long as human labor, communications, institutions, and some capital were intact, the tremendous physical loss was not crucial.

The drive to restore the environment as it was before, to re-create an image of the past, is quite evident. It had roots both practical and psychological. A major reorganization of the City was never seriously considered (despite the fantasies of later historians on this subject). Rebuilding was rapid and vigorous because each man could start again on his own familiar land. Street widenings were strongly contested not only because of the resultant loss of land but in fear of increased traffic or of change itself. New public open space was constantly in danger of encroachment by buildings or of illegal use as work yards or dumping grounds. The parish churches were rebuilt on their previous ground plans. Old forms and ceremonies were reestablished as quickly as possible. Scarce time and cash were expended on symbolic actions: the reconstruction of St. Paul's, the erection of a Monument to the Fire, the building of elaborate new guildhalls, and the holding of a ceremonial royal feast among the ruins, complete with drums and banners, to mark the start of work on the new Exchange. The ruins themselves were depressing and thought dangerous. Construction became a good in itself—a subject for sermons. How the new buildings might be used and occupied was a question that followed later.

The images and feelings of Londoners in the aftermath of this massive crisis are hard to reconstruct from the historical documents, though the first vivid descriptions of the terror and panic of the burning are eloquent enough. The disaster left a better physical city, clearly. Traffic was eased, though not for long. Plague had been recurrent, but there would be no more epidemics until the cholera of the nineteenth century. And a major fire never recurs in the burned-out districts. The houses were much safer and more commodious, the streets clean and firm. On the other hand, the resultant strain on declining medieval institutions probably hastened their collapse, and the historic shift in the spatial structure of economy and population was further stimulated. Just as with redevelopment today, the poor were driven out of the city center. London capital was poured into the rebuilding, and a slowdown of London trade briefly showed the effect. But the long-term result was more likely a stimulus, owing to the more rapid dissolution of the guilds.

In any event, the tale of recovery is well remembered. After its disastrous earthquake of 1923, Tokyo sent to ask how London had met the Fire.

Bath: The Preserved City

The city of Bath, built as an aristocratic health resort within a span of seventy years in the eighteenth century, is still a miraculous whole—our best remaining example of a Georgian town. Images of it appear in every standard text on city design; it attracts 300,000 tourists every year. Its unique visual qualities, its architectural importance, its representation of a particular period in British social history, its romantic associations, all make it a special legacy.

Reference 34

Its problems today are equally special, reminiscent of those in many other historic areas, though in Bath inflated. There are 2818 buildings officially listed for preservation in the city, or one for every twenty-eight inhabitants. The homogeneous building stock is homogeneously obsolete. Forty percent of the floor space in the central area is vacant, and

Figure 1
The fine facade of Ralph
Allen's house in Bath, seen
from crowded service
alleys to the rear.

Figure 2
The rooftops of Bath reveal
its problems of structural
decay.

much of the remainder above the ground floor is in only nominal use. Interiors are ill suited for contemporary activities. Speculators built Bath, and their principle was ostentation. The thin stone walls and light frames are in poor condition, exaggerated by deferred maintenance. The handsome Georgian plaster ceilings offer no resistance to fire. Were ordinary legal standards strictly applied, Bath would have to be rebuilt.

While the predicted growth of the city will create severe demands for land for expansion, the residential use of the center has been declining, and its substandard dwelling units are occupied by old, poor tenants. Remodeling would drive these tenants out and would probably require substantial subsidies in any case. And who would be attracted to live in the remodeled apartments? Hotels, large shops, and new offices are sorely needed, and they now tend to locate in areas not subject to architectural control. There is some danger that commercial enterprises not oriented to the tourist may move out of the city altogether. Yet it is the lively, colorful center, even more than the impressive but rather lifeless Georgian terraces, which is the principal tourist attraction. Access and parking are difficult, and adequate provision for the new traffic will require two tunnels and a network of primary roads at a cost well beyond ordinary national yardsticks for such improvements.

Bath could be allowed to continue its slow physical decline, paradoxically squeezed by its steady population growth, until some more violent readjustment took place. Or massive renewal could be undertaken to serve the new needs, though it would be sure to damage Bath's unique character. Or large subsidies might preserve the city as a national treasure, a policy that could only be expected to accelerate its transition to an elegant tourist encampment. No other use has yet been found for the center that can be accommodated without destruction of the existing landscape.

For tourists or visiting professionals the scene is magnificent on a fine day: the green setting, the harmonious stone terraces, a leisurely air, the sense of a place long inhabited. Popular postcard views fix the importance of particular visual memories: the

Abbey through the Stall Street colonnade; the green hills from the city center, seen over the Orange Grove and the Avon. But the town, like a stage set, lacks the historic depth and living presence that is felt in an active, complex city.

What does this unique place mean to its visitor: the Roman baths underground, the bright shops, some famous views, and the house where Nelson dallied with Lady Hamilton? How do the residents themselves look at their city? With affection? With frustration? With a cool economic eye? What should they be willing to sacrifice to preserve it? Indeed, what *should* it mean to them, for Bath was built by the rents wrung from an exploited peasantry and out of the profits of the mills?

Stoke-on-Trent: Industrial Wasteland

Reference 37

The industrial towns of England are the underside of Bath. The village potteries of North Staffordshire had the geological advantage of a great variety of throwing clays located on a rich coalfield. During the seventeenth century as internal trade developed, those local potteries came to dominate the Midlands market. During the eighteenth century new techniques for making fine porcelain converted the craft shops into large industrial establishments, and the original cluster of six potting villages grew together to become Stoke-on-Trent. Now the dark row houses run over long ridges, between the monumental waste heaps and abandoned pits of old industrial workings. Twenty percent of the built-up area of Stoke is derelict land. The heaps are the by-products of coal lifted from deep shafts and of the pottery marl extracted from open pits. The coal mines are closing now, but ceramics continues to prosper and steadily enlarges its diggings. Waste in the potteries is particularly voluminous; much of the total mass of the materials processed is left on the land, partly as waste sand, partly as broken or defective chinaware. Sand and shards, being chemically stable, are permanent additions to the landscape. The pits are slowly enlarged, but finally they are dug or collapse down to the water table, which is polluted by the acid seepage of the tips. The canals and branch rail lines that wove this industrial landscape together are falling into disuse. Rights-of-way have been abandoned, bridges dismantled, old tunnels blocked up. Since pottery production remained largely unchanged into the 1930s, works were simply added to and not rebuilt. Now they must be reconstructed, and their empty bottle ovens and domed kilns are disappearing, along with the towering pitheads of the mines.

The landscape is harsh and lunar, eloquent of the misery and injustice of the industrial revolution. Yet there is also a grandeur in these gigantic and varicolored heaps, some bare, some coated with grass, which loom like great volcanic cones over the house ridges. The high pit hoists and slender stacks, the low domes and fat brick bottles of the kilns are remarkable forms. The massive brickwork of the bridges, canals, and railway cuttings are handsome engineering surfaces. The derelict land itself, which weaves through the entire urban fabric, is a resource of a special kind. Already it is used for picnics, for walks and sunbathing, for games and adventures—a wilderness retreat in the heart of the city.

The city, using national funds, is resolved to rehabilitate this landscape of waste. The prime motives are undoubtedly psychological and political: to change the image of industrial spoliation, to hold its emigrating youth, to attract new enterprise, to erase the unloved past. The strategy is to clear away old structures, level the land, plant it in grass and trees, turn it into standard parks or industrial sites. Cedric Price has proposed a "Potteries Thinkbelt," a system of mobile teaching facilities parked along the old railroad lines and sidings, students being housed throughout the community. Young designers see other possibilities: the canals may become new tourist routes, the railway lines linear fairgrounds or housing, the tips sports mountains, the deep pits vertical pleasure grounds, the pools and marshes preserves for nature study. They dream of kilns and mines put to new uses, the beautiful forms of the gasholders and pit machinery preserved and enhanced. (Today in the United States many central-city living areas are being abandoned, becoming wastelands of another kind. Much of this land is falling back into public hands. Will we have the courage and the sense to see this as an opportunity and not simply a disaster?)

Figure 3
Stoke-on-Trent from the
air. The terrace houses are
set among workshops and
barren lots, but the bottle
kilns are magnificent.

Figure 4
Broken crockery, the
indestructible by-product
of the kilns.

Figure 5
The gigantic waste heaps
of the collieries command
the scene.

Figure 6
The flooded marl pits
make a new wilderness.

Meanwhile, the industrial archaeologist is dismayed to see the remains of a critical historical period so casually swept away. The people of Stoke themselves seem to be of two minds: wishing to forget their past but also taking a certain grim pride in it, feeling a sense of survival and accomplishment. To them, the tips are almost natural features, adding drama to the city. But who asks the people what their man-made mountains mean to them and how they would like them changed?

Ciudad Guayana: A New City

Reference 25

The Guayana is the Venezuelan frontier: an empty interior of mountains, savanna, and forest, drained by the Orinoco River. The name itself speaks of adventure and gossiped riches of gold and diamonds. The Guayana is also a region of extraordinary real resources in iron and other metals. It has deepwater access to the ocean, great reserves of timber, and abundant waterpower. As a nation, Venezuela has experienced an average growth of its real gross product of 7 percent every year for the past thirty years—one of the highest rates of economic growth so long sustained of any nation in modern times. Growth was based on oil, and with growth came the breakup of a feudal society, an inmigration of foreigners, a leap in domestic population, and the dramatic flow of rural people into the cities of the coast and of the intermontane valleys above the coasts. The deep interior remained largely empty.

The liberal junta that overthrew a traditional landowner oligarchy in 1945 sought independence from the domination of oil and foreign capital. It wanted to build a modern industrial economy, and the discovery of iron-ore deposits in the Guayana in 1947 turned its attention there. Dependence might be converted into autonomy by "sowing the petroleum"—investing the profits from oil to build a new and diversified economy. The reactionary coup of Marcos Pérez Jiménez in 1948 extinguished these projects of comprehensive regional development, but after his overthrow ten years later they were revived.

The Corporación Venezolana de Guayana (CVG) was formed in 1960 to develop the resources of the Guayana, focusing particularly on a site at the confluence of the Orinoco and the Caroní. It was at this site, under the Pérez Jiménez dictatorship, that a small dam had been built, two U.S. steel corporations had established plants to concentrate iron ore for export, and a nationally owned steel mill was under construction.

The location is a magnificent one: dry, gently sloping uplands bordered by the two rivers—the gigantic Orinoco and the Caroní—the smaller one tumbling over its dramatic falls just before its junction with the parent river. The climate is hot, but a cool breeze blows. Though the vegetation generally is sparse, there is thick tropical growth along the riverbanks. On the east was the old colonial town of San Felix; on the west, fifteen miles away, the new steel mill was rising. In between, at the mouth of the Caroní, were the two iron-ore plants, one with its associated company village of Puerto Ordaz.

In 1936 there were 1000 persons in the area and by 1950 still only 4000. But by 1961, when the CVG entered the scene as chief landowner, developer, and operator of the steel mill, there were already 42,000 people there. One-third of them were housed in self-built shacks, west of San Felix or near Puerto Ordaz. To provide the labor force for the projected industrial development, the future city —Ciudad Guayana—was to grow to a size that was variously estimated as being between 250,000 and 600,000 people. Ten percent of the public investment of the nation was to be diverted into creating a new Guayana.

Immigrants were pouring in to find work in this boom area. Most of them had come upriver from the coastal towns and farms of eastern Venezuela: farmers, fishermen, oilmen, rivermen, miners— single men and women, families, women with their children, men who had left their families behind. They were ready to join the modern world. They were practical in their orientation, willing to move and to learn, and their social structure was elastic. One-half of them had been unemployed, and one-third were still unemployed after a month in the new city. But they had heard of the possibility of work, and they knew someone in Ciudad Guayana who might help them to survive until they found it. They complained about the hard conditions of life in the new city—they would have preferred Caracas —but were optimistic about the future, and very few chose to leave. They expected and desired change.

A smaller group of in-migrants came from Caracas or from abroad—the middle-class technicians and professionals to staff the mills and serve the city. Lured by wages and perhaps by the promise of adventure, they were highly critical of Ciudad Guayana. Almost half of these people were foreign nationals. Few looked on residence here as more than a brief interlude in their lives.

The city grew rapidly over the extended and broken site—a spread of bustling, resident-built settlements peppered with a few planned housing projects, schools, hospitals, and major roads. Industries gathered around the steel mill far to the west; commerce boomed in San Felix and in a spontaneous center at the edge of Puerto Ordaz. Population rose from 42,000 in 1961 to 50,000 in 1962, to 73,000 in 1965, and to almost 90,000 in 1966.

The CVG struggled to create a coherent plan for the development of the area and to provide the necessary infrastructure of roads, utilities, and services. Everything was in short supply. Housing lagged critically, low-income housing in particular. Of 3600 dwelling units built in 1962–1965 by the CVG or its associated agencies, only 200 were intended for occupants from the lowest income levels who formed the bulk of the in-migrants. By 1965, 45 percent of the occupied dwellings were self-built shacks. Surveyed lots for these shacks were provided to channel this growth and prevent it from inundating reserved sites, but even this program met less than half the demand. The migrants were solving their own housing problem, even if contrary to plan.

Physical planning labored under the pressure of events but also under many uncertainties. Economic forecasts shifted, and the estimated scale of the future city leaped from 150,000 to 600,000 inhabitants and then subsided to 300,000 again. As planners learned more about the probable economic organization, the site, and the needs of the inhabitants, the form of the city metamorphosed from a series of settlements to a single large city and then to a linear development. The planned center of gravity moved jerkily westward from San Felix toward the steel mill, each leap raising new problems for the professionals. Previous decisions and actions accumulated as illogical restraints on each new plan. Field engineers pushed ahead to get the job done. The squatter settlements expanded steadily. Within the planning staff, each division battled for its own viewpoint, and the top administration cautiously masked its ultimate decisions. How to respond to immediate issues in planning and yet also attend to the future is still a mystery to the planning trade.

The planning was done in Caracas, three hundred miles away, out of contact with site and settlers. Remoteness was reinforced by a tradition of central control and local dependence, of distrust and even disdain for local people. The planners lived in a symbolic world of maps. Their view of the city was extended, abstract, and privileged. It encompassed the entire elongated district; it penetrated the empty lands and was conscious of the surrounding natural features and their potentials. It glossed over the diversity of human settlements. Planners lived in the long future and saw the city as a coherent entity struggling to be born, constantly threatened by the chaotic actions of local people.

People living on the site viewed it quite differently. They also looked to the future, but a future growing directly out of the activities they could see immediately around them rather than a distant vision of a city of half a million. Their view of the place was concrete and particular, fixed on the inhabited areas and not on the natural site, sharply conscious of the particular characteristics of the numerous barrios and settlements. Ciudad Guayana was not a single urban unit to them. Indeed, most of them had never heard of the place.

Of course, they were aware of change. The rapid current of Venezuelan history is visible to everyone. In Ciudad Guayana, at least, change was welcome: 98 percent of the residents thought that the city was changing for the better, and 80 percent wanted the city to grow even faster. "It will transform itself into a great city," they said. Everything new was good. To the inhabitants the CVG was not the orchestrator of the growth of this new city but a distant organization that, along with other agencies, created some roads, built some dams and hospitals, and also perversely blocked the rise of new commercial enterprises or the acquisition of certain house sites.

The newest migrants learned the city rapidly in their search for economic opportunity. Even those who were familiar with this changing city had to concentrate on absorbing new information. And so the older inhabitants knew the city somewhat less well than the newer ones. The poorer people, although they may have had trouble in putting the city together in an intellectually coherent schema, nevertheless knew it better than the technicians in their affluent ghettos.

Although the westward extension of Ciudad Guayana toward the mill was well-settled official policy, the people were unaware of the symbolic futures on planners' maps. They predicted growth in all directions. They did not seem to give much thought to the new center of the city on Alta Vista that the professionals had visualized. Over half the people believed that Ciudad Guayana might merge with Ciudad Bolívar, forty miles away. They could not imagine where a new bridge and road were going. They seemed to bypass the settlement of Castillito; thus the small entrepreneurs were building in that area even as the new crossing was cutting off their access. People struggled on foot through a park to reach the old crossing at Castillito from the new highway, and finally their protests forced the construction of a link from that highway. Thus the future image of the inhabitants scored a round; now even the fate of the proposed main shopping center at Alta Vista is in doubt. Although a public office to disseminate future plans was established in 1965, it was oriented to visiting experts and developers, not to the citizens.

This city of migrants is a city of hope and energy but also of uncertainty and some misgivings. Many families have been able to enter the industrial economy by learning on the job or by building small houses to sell or rent or by opening a small

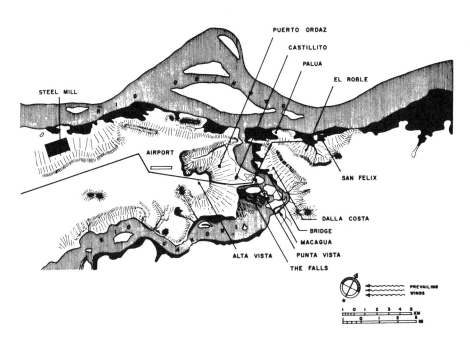

PUERTO ORDAZ
CASTILLITO
PALUA
EL ROBLE
STEEL MILL
AIRPORT
SAN FELIX
DALLA COSTA
BRIDGE
MACAGUA
ALTA VISTA   PUNTA VISTA
THE FALLS

PREVAILING
WINDS

Figure 7
The impressive topo-
graphic setting of Ciudad
Guayana: sixteen miles of
the south bank of the
Orinoco River at its con-
fluence with the Caroní.
This is the professional's
view of the new city.

Figure 8
Maps of Ciudad Guayana
drawn by its residents.
Note the diversity of styles
and yet how these images
emphasize roads and set-
tlements, ignoring the
great rivers.

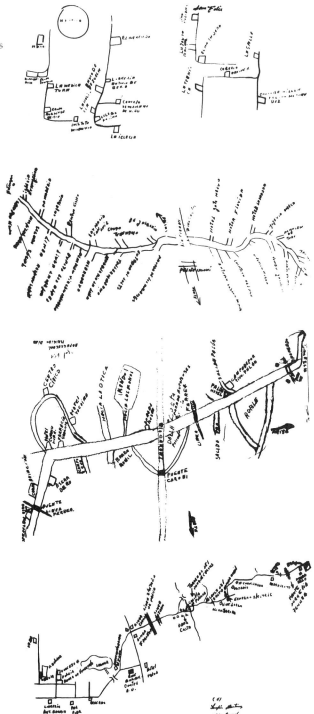

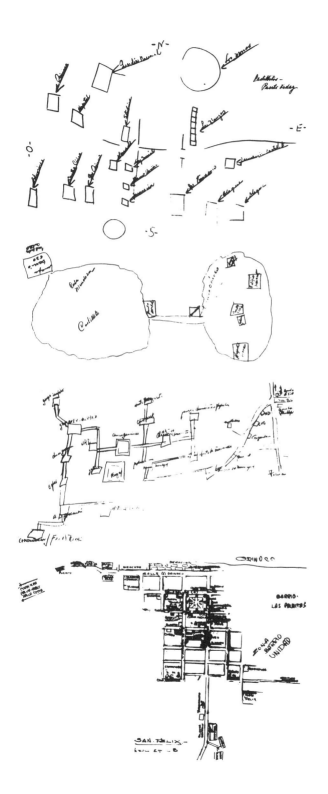

23

business. But unemployment has been severe: over 20 percent in 1961, falling to 12 percent in 1968. Even so, there has been a marked upward shift in income, quality of housing, and nature of occupation for the new arrivals to Ciudad Guayana. Two-thirds of these migrants now own real estate. In the barrios they can see many of their neighbors rising out of poverty. Most of them believe that unemployment and ranchos will be eliminated. Will events justify the hopes?

At present the squatter settlements, with their wide mix of class and race and their steady pace of physical improvement, are to be found everywhere in the city—in sharp contrast to their forced separation from the planned city of Brasília, for example. But residential segregation in Ciudad Guayana is apparently growing, with the Caroní acting as a dividing line. Will later arrivals find that the ladders of opportunity have been withdrawn? As construction levels off, what substitutes can be found for the economic advancement it now makes possible? How can jobs be created for women, who are the mainstays of the fluid families? Can the migrants' children get to school or acquire books? Is a dual economy, a permanent underclass, developing here, as elsewhere in Venezuela?

When forward-looking planning controls were imposed on the land, they simultaneously reduced the possibility of local participation. How can the new city remain flexible and receptive to individual energy and still have enough certainty and coherence to be understandable? In the short run, how can the social transition be made easy? In the longer run, will the city and the society continue to justify the optimistic energy that is building them?

Havana:
Container for
Social Revolution

The aim of building communism in one leap is transforming Cuba. As a container of that transformation, the colonial city of Havana resists it but also provides the accumulation of capital to carry the revolution through its critical early stages. The Havana environment reflects this sudden displacement in unique ways.

The city contains almost a quarter of the people of the nation. In the old walled town and central area two-and three-story tenements, with shop fronts on the ground, are densely packed together. Scarcely a tree breaks the force of the tropical sun. Farther out, the former middle-class areas are a jumble of single-family houses, apartment buildings, and overgrown gardens, much like the older sections of Los Angeles. Tall modern apartments and luxury hotels cluster near the sea in Vedado. Not far away are the monumental buildings of government. Next to the port and its industries, and in the old rural towns swallowed by metropolitan growth, are the shantytowns and crowded dwellings of the poor. The sea has many colors, the clouds pile up dramatically, the sun is hot and the air heavy with humidity and fumes. At night the city sparkles. In these ways Havana is like many a Latin American metropolis.

In the early colonial days Havana was an isolated trading fortress, the assembly point for the annual convoy to Spain and the legal monopolist of Caribbean trade and power. Once the indigenous Indians had been killed, 50 percent of the island's population lived in the city. As sugar and tobacco prospered, the rest of the island gradually developed. However, the subsequent concentration of finance and export agriculture in foreign ownership brought on a recentralization in the metropolis. Cuban society, Cuban culture, along with its technicians, business, and industry were all centered in Havana. The middle class moved out along the axis of the beach. Displaced peasants poured in to build shanties on the fringes. Land prices soared, and fortunes were built on speculation. American tourists flew in, attracted by sun and sea, the gambling casinos, the glittering night life, the superficial taste of Latin American culture. The national plan predicted a Havana of four million by the year 2000.

The revolutionary army entered the city in January 1959, and the subsequent changes were rapid. The middle classes fled, leaving large areas of the city vacant. A blockade stopped the normal importation of materials and equipment. Rents were reduced in half by decree, and then the housing was given to its tenants. Much land was nationalized, and land prices were pegged at a low level. Land speculation suddenly ceased.

Reference 65

Some new apartments were built by the revolutionary government, to begin the rehousing of slum dwellers and to absorb the large pool of urban unemployed, but they proved costly. There were miscalculations in planning; and the concentration of slum families raised familiar social problems. As unemployment changed into labor shortage, one motive for large-scale building evaporated. New construction in the city was sharply curtailed and was redirected toward schools, clinics, and nurseries.

Internal barriers broke down; private control of access to the sea and its beaches disappeared. The economic filters that regulated entry into areas of better housing dissolved, although the tendency to remain permanently in rent-free apartments perpetuates many of the old characteristics of population distribution. Private clubs were converted into public restaurants and social centers. The luxury district of hotels and tall apartments in Vedado, once restricted to tourists and the Cuban upper class, is now the cultural and entertainment center for the entire city. In the evenings, Vedado's streets are full of people, promenading or queuing up at movies, restaurants, or ice cream parlors. The administrative center has mushroomed, shifting toward Vedado. Offices move frequently from one remodeled house or apartment to another. The Miramar seaside suburbs, left largely vacant by the middle class, were reoccupied by some 100,000 students, brought in on scholarship from the entire nation.

The former capitol is a museum; the old walled city—while still occupied by houses, warehouses, and small offices—has lost most of its shops and large offices. Faded signs still hang over the former central shopping streets, and pedestrians still move along them during the day. But the ground-floor frontages are partly deserted; the glass fronts are dark or screened off for shabby offices or light industry. The nationalized stores, displaying scanty goods on dusty shelves, are few. People wait patiently in line outside the local food stores. The distribution of goods is no longer the prime, or the most glamorous, central-city function.

These changes were sharpened by shifts in national policy. In a period of economic stringency, when it was a central aim to reduce previous inequalities of geography and class, investment in Havana was suspended in favor of building the agricultural base. The prediction for Havana's population by 2000 is now two instead of four million. Its rapid growth has subsided to a slower pace of increase (although it has by no means ceased), owing to the effects of the rural investment program and a stern control of ration cards, whose validity is restricted to geographical districts. No new construction occurs in the city, except in the port or for essential schools, clinics, factories, or administrative buildings.

The physical plant is slowly wearing down: buses are inadequate, and it takes much time to move across the city; utilities sometimes fail; buildings are not maintained. While the construction of new buildings in the countryside is rapidly being industrialized, no thought has yet been given to the rationalization of building maintenance in the city or to the renewal of the usable housing stock. Tenant-owners, however, may be seen patching and repairing their quarters with materials they have scraped up from some doubtful source. Construction rubble lies in the streets. Half the citizens of Havana are still badly housed; the visual surfaces are pallid, shabby, and worn. Traffic is light, but it is noisy and smoking. The contrast is startling between the vitality of the people on the streets—well fed and adequately clothed—and the exhaustion of the physical setting. Another striking contrast is the absence of advertising—our accustomed gaudy surface of color and images.

Sweeping changes have occurred just outside the city, rather than within it. A massive force of city labor has been mobilized to convert the wastelands around Havana into a vast city garden, the so-called Cordón. Three hundred thousand hectares have been planted in coffee or citrus fruits or devoted to intensive cattle raising, by using eight million man-days of weekend and voluntary labor. Earth dams across the intermittent watercourses have made a score of new lakes among the agricultural plantations. The lakes store irrigation water and recharge the hard-pressed city water table, but they are also used for boating, fishing, and picknicking. The Cordón is a new landscape at a vast scale: open, parklike, tended. The strongest motive for building it is undoubtedly ideological: to bring city people into contact with the country and with rural labor, to give them a sense of communal achievement, to integrate work and leisure. Visually, the country begins to reach back into the city.

In the southwest, at that edge of the city, the huge new Lenin Park is being rushed to completion on land rescued from speculation. It contains two artificial lakes, many restaurants and picnic grounds, a library, an aquarium, a water theater, sports grounds, riding trails, its own passenger railroad. It is liberally planted with "instant" forests. Several old houses, a Spanish ruin, and an abandoned quarry have all been ingeniously reused. Its 1600 acres have been planned to accommodate 65,000 persons a day. This new landscape, with its new activities (like horseback riding), will open up novel opportunities for the people's leisure.

Activities are shifting rapidly within an inherited physical container. How can this major social transition be made without wasting all the character and useful capital of the past? How can the environment be made flexible and receptive, qualities essential in an experimental society?

From brief conversations, one feels that the people of Havana are proud of their city, once beautiful, now shabby, but destined to be beautiful again. They are aware of its inconveniences but look forward to future improvements. But does the city express these new aspirations—point forward to the new social and spatial possibilities? Or does it only point back to the comforts and injustices of the past? Perhaps the physical Havana of today not only resists change but also displays the wrong models of past styles of living.

Disaster, preservation, renewal, growth, revolution—each of these characteristic transformations presents different problems for managing the environment. Common to them all is the perception of change—not only those objective alterations in the state of things but what we understand them to be and how they connect with our hopes and memories and sense of time's flow.

The Presence of the Past

2

Throughout the world, but particularly in the economically advanced countries, fragments of an obsolete physical environment are lovingly preserved, or restored so that they may be preserved, as relics of time gone by. Such preservation is costly not only because it involves direct outlays of money and time but also because piecemeal retention causes endless difficulties for new development. In building a new library, for example, the Harvard Graduate School of Education recently paid $500,000 to move two rather small, old houses a few hundred feet.

Fierce political battles are fought over whether a building or set of buildings should be saved, since different groups place widely varying values on the remains. Because of the fixed and bulky nature of the objects and the strong personal attachments they arouse, their preservation is a far more strident affair than the preservation of movable objects, records, or customs. Nevertheless the resistance to the loss of historical environment is today becoming more determined as affluence increases and physical change itself is more rapid. And no wonder, since the past is known, familiar, a possession in which we may feel secure.

Environmental preservation, at least as a widespread and coherent doctrine, is fairly new. Medieval masons razed an old building without a qualm, even though old, "historic" structures were then much rarer than now. In Tudor inventories, chattels called "old" were put at the foot of the list, implying they had little value. In Western Europe, at least, the idea of preservation first appeared about 1500, in the form of an esoteric attraction to relict buildings, even to the point of the construction of sham ruins. By the eighteenth century an affection for the structures of the past was a widespread upper-class fashion, and by the nineteenth century it became part of the intellectual baggage of all middle-class travelers. In the same century, first in the United States and slightly later in Europe, organized movements sprang up to preserve historic landmarks for the public.

In the United States the first efforts were

Preservation's Past

Reference 61

directed at saving particular buildings, especially the houses associated with patriotic figures. Reinforcing national solidarity and pride was the chief reason for preservation. Specific motives ranged from attempts to prevent disunity before the Civil War and to reestablish it afterward, through the concern for "Americanizing" the immigrant, to the moves to magnify patriotic feelings during the twentieth-century wars. Relying on history to maintain coherence and common purpose in moments of stress and disunity is a familiar human tendency. The militant interest in black history is its most recent manifestation in America.

Later this patriotic emphasis merged with the enthusiasm for ruins of the romantic tradition, and architectural restoration became a basic principle of the movement. Connection with an established historic event and the quality of a building remain even today the chief criteria for preservation. The scientific motives of archaeology and the economic ones of tourist promotion appeared somewhat later. Perhaps most recently of all, in the United States at least, large segments of the population have come to feel that preservation is moral in itself and that environments rich in such features are more pleasant places in which to live. Patriotism and literary glamour have defined certain classic periods whose traces are most worth preserving: the late colonial and Revolutionary years in New England, the brief episode of pioneering in the forested interior, the antebellum days in the South, the period of exploration and cattle raising on the Great Plains (which passed so quickly), the mining era in the Western mountains, the years of the Spanish colonies in the Southwest, and, of course, the undefined background of the scattered and "timeless" Indian. Preservation has usually been the work of established middle- and upper-class citizens. The history enshrined in museums is chosen and interpreted by those who give the dollars.

Environments rich in historic remains often follow a particular pattern: once markedly prosperous, they then suffered a rapid economic decline and remained stagnant for long periods, though continuing to be occupied and at least partially maintained. Many now charming New England towns and farming areas were well-to-do in the early 1800s but in the later years of the century sank into the trough of the westward wave of national expansion. This stagnation must then be followed by a second period of wealth (whether belonging to the region itself or brought in by visitors) that can bear the costs of preservation.

The pattern can be seen not only in those small towns and rural regions that have decayed and then revived but also in the inner parts of large cities that have stagnated while the total urban region continued to prosper. Boston's Back Bay is one example of many. Natural decay is destructive of unoccupied old environment, but active development by subsequent generations is a far more rapid agent of disposal. And since if anything is preserved it tends to be the most expensive or most imposing or most symbolic of some classic period, the preserved environments tend to be very limited in extent. They represent the continuum of time in a spasmodic way and give a distorted view of the past since they are composed of the buildings of prosperous classes in prosperous times—times, furthermore, that quickly passed away. Such remains only reinforce that misguided view of history which sees it as consisting of sharp peaks of achievement separated by long, empty durations.

There are several ways of dealing with a valued piece of an old environment. What remains can simply be saved from destruction, perhaps by moving it away from danger. It can be restored by minor repairs and refurbishings. Or it can be rebuilt in as careful a copy of its "original" state as is currently known. This may be done with original material, judiciously pieced out and refinished, or with covert new material, or even with obviously new material. Put another way, the patina of time may be retained, imitated, or removed. When there is a frank and complete reconstruction, using new material, on a new site, the aim may be an appearance of having just been built, an aim that may be carried out even to the details of equipment and perhaps the use of costumed actors. Such a reconstruction will often shock contemporary taste (Greek tem-

Preservation Battle Lines

Reference 31

ples were gaudily painted in their day), and sometimes it will be made ridiculous by subsequent scholarship. But it can be a strong evocation of the past for a general audience.

The official priority rankings of historical societies usually range from the least to the most disturbance, that is, from preservation through restoration, reconstitution, and relocation to complete reconstruction. But this simple formula cloaks many subtleties and invites controversies. What, for example, happens to later historical additions to the original structure? Since historic structures are thought of as having been built all at one time and then potentially eternal, but have actually undergone a continuous process of physical change and human occupation, and since our view of history itself changes constantly, the controversies may be heated and scholastic. Robert Scott's Antarctic hut, unused since his fatal expedition sixty years ago, survives intact in the polar cold: papers, food, and equipment are just as they were. The effect is powerful—it corresponds to our wish to arrest the past—but we cannot easily reproduce the circumstances that created it.

Sometimes the historical object is reconstructed at regular intervals, preserving not the old materials but rather the ancient form. The 2000-year outline of the White Horse of Uffington is still visible on the downs because it is renewed by its annual "scouring." The temple at Ise, completely rebuilt with new material on a new site every twenty years, conserves the most primitive form of any building in Japan. Such periodic reconstructions, because they do not depend on a single effort, evade some of the issues posed here.

According to another doctrine, only the external historical shell need be preserved or reconstructed. It can then shelter current, active uses, and internal physical modifications suitable to those new uses are allowable. "Outsides" are public, historic, and regulated, while "insides" are private, fluid, and free. An aversion to an unused or "museum" environment is connected with this doctrine. Even then, there are difficult decisions to be made: the interior-exterior dichotomy is a convenient distinction to make, but

Figure 9
The metamorphosis of a house: the Henry Hotchkiss house, built on Chapel Street, New Haven, Connecticut, in 1841–1842, as it looked in 1857,

and in 1865, with a new story, ironwork, and paint,

and in its most recent form, assumed in 1960.

Figure 10
A car is elevated for lubri-
cation at the altar of this
old Italian church.

Figure 11
The temple at Ise is rebuilt
exactly as before on the
alternate site every twentieth year. The structures
are always immaculately
new, yet they faithfully
conserve the ancient form.

what kinds of specific modifications are, in fact, allowable? In restoring the Nash terraces around Regent's Park in London for modern offices, the facades were rebuilt according to the original designs, but enough of the former internal arrangement was also imposed so that the view from the street would have the right sense of depth. How far can we go in subsidizing activities that are likely to survive in preserved surroundings? To what degree does contemporary utility, however discreetly provided, rupture the sense of historical integrity? The ceramic bathrooms of colonial Williamsburg come as a shock. And what is to be done where inside and outside are hard to separate, as in a large public building or in a landscape?

Strict preservation is the more pessimistic view. It considers any reconstruction as fraudulent and thinks of time as a process of regrettable but inevitable dissolution. We can protect only what still remains by a variety of means, principally passive but including removal to a protected place (then the loss of the museum itself can erase the concentrated harvest of generations!). The object to be preserved can be presented for better public view, but the process of decay is only slowed down—not stopped.

One may also take a purely intellectual view, aiming to learn as much and as accurately about the past as possible and only secondarily to preserve, use, or exhibit it. One is then justified in destroying remains by dissection or excavation or in reburying them then after inspection so that they are kept intact for later generations of scientists, even though they may not then be seen or used by the general public.

As vexing as the doctrine of preservation is the definition of its purpose. What pieces of the environment should we attempt to reconstruct or preserve, and what are the warrants for historical treatment? Are we looking for evidence of the climactic moments or for any manifestation of tradition we can find, or are we judging and evaluating the past, choosing the more significant over the less, retaining what we think of as best? Should things be saved because they were associated with important persons or events? Because they are unique or nearly so or, quite the contrary, because they were most typical of their time? Because of their importance as a group symbol? Because of their intrinsic qualities in the present? Because of their special usefulness as sources of intellectual information about the past? Or should we simply (as we most often do) let chance select for us and preserve for a second century everything that has happened to survive the first?

Such issues spring from confusions about how the past is perceived and what the nature of the endless process of environmental change is, as well as from disagreements about the purpose of preservation. Memory cannot retain everything; if it could, we would be overwhelmed with data. Memory is the result of a process of selection and of organizing what is selected so that it is within reach in expectable situations. There must also be some random accumulations to enable us to discover unexpected relationships. But serendipity is possible only when recollection is essentially a holding fast to what is meaningful and a release of what is not.

Every thing, every event, every person is "historic." To attempt to preserve all of the past would be life-denying. We dispose of physical evidences of the past for the same reason that we forget. To someone interested in action or understanding in the present, the past is irrelevant if a description of the present furnishes him with a better or more concise analysis on which he can base his action. Past events are indeed often relevant to present possibilities. They may explain causes or point to likely outcomes. Or they may give us a sense of proportion to help us bear our present difficulties. But these causes and probabilities must be created and disentangled from the heap of history. Indeed, there may be old wrongs and hatreds that are quite relevant to actions today, but from which the present must be severed.

Reference 16

Reference 67

"Man," Nietzsche said, "must have the strength to break up the past." "History is a nightmare from which I am trying to awake," cried Stephen Dedalus in *Ulysses*. New environments are often sought as escapes from servitude to the past, even if the freedom found thereby is sometimes less complete than it promised to be, and even if many valuable memories are lost in the severing. We prefer to select and create our past and to make it part of the living present.

Thus there must be a way of disposing of obsolete objects. According to a survey made in 1936, most buildings in London other than the relatively few recognized "historic" ones were, on the average, renewed in thirty years and abandoned in sixty. The rate of replacement in the central sections of American cities is faster. In dense settlements, where needs and opportunities constantly change, we cannot depend on natural decay or abandonment as a means of dispensing with the unwanted environment. Nor is disposal by small building units effective when a major change is desired since new development must then fit into an unyielding framework. Even final abandonment may sterilize space for subsequent use, because of the cost of re-forming and reusing the derelict area. And since abandonment is also usually by small increments, the process of desertion is commonly prolonged and painful for those left behind.

If we have been reasonably successful at junking environment in those most active central areas of our cities, where the intensity of new activity can support the cost of piecemeal removal, and also in the low-density fringes, where disposal is cheap, elsewhere in North American cities we have been much less successful, wherever the wanted change is more than a gradual improvement for an unchanging activity. Under the banner of historical preservation, we have saved many isolated buildings of doubtful significance or present quality, which are out of context with their surroundings and without a means of supporting their use or maintenance or of communicating their meaning to the public. At the same time, in urban renewal, we wipe out substantial areas of used environment at great psychological and social cost, to be replaced by new settings that lack many desirable features of the old. Having suffered the pangs of uprooting and saddened by the inhuman quality of much of the new urban development, many of us conclude that it is time to stop growth and change, or at least to leave the older areas alone and concentrate growth in the "empty" fringes. But the settled areas change in any event, and still the

Disposal

Reference 74

environment does not adapt quickly enough to new economic and social demands.

Designers are aware that it is easier to plan when there are some commitments than it is when the situation is completely open. The building in the hills, the house in a dense city, and the interior in an old building are easier to create, and often more interesting and apt in their solution, than are their counterparts on flat plains, in open land, and in a new structure. The fixed characteristics restrict the range of possible solutions and therefore ease the agony of the design search. In addition, the accidental background permits solutions that are rich in form and full of contrast. Clearly, this is true only where the fixed elements are somehow valuable and do not completely inhibit desirable alteration. It is interesting to redesign the interior of an old warehouse for apartments, but not if the massive walls have no windows, or the ceiling heights are extremely low, or the rooms are perpetually damp. Nonphysical restraints may have similar effects. The unique institutions, values, or behavior of a group of users can be used as a principal source of strong character in a solution.

In an analogous way, older communities that have grown slowly have certain advantages for the inhabitant over new settlements. The older towns tend to be richer and more complex, with choices, services, and attachments better fitted to the plurality of needs and values of a diverse population. People will resist forcible removal from these older settlements, and signs of social stress often appear in the early days of the new towns to which they have moved. New housing can often be inserted more happily into existing communities than it can be erected on open ground since the former action can be taken without destroying the social fabric or losing access to the web of facilities.

Designers themselves are often found living in old houses in old districts, unless they have chosen to inflict their own personal designs on themselves. When they occupy old houses, however, they do not simply preserve them; they modify them by suppression and addition to enliven the surviving elements. Longevity and evanescence gain savor in each other's presence: "In a gourd that had been handed down for three centuries, a flower that would fade in a morning." The old environment is seen as an opportunity for dramatic enhancement and becomes richer than it was. This is not preservation, or even simple addition, but a particular use of old and new.

Reference 69

It is the familiar connections, not all the old physical things themselves, that people want to retain, except where those things have a *personal* connection: their own furniture, the family mementos. One of the problems of the large new suburban communities is how to maintain some continuity of image and association despite the physical and social upheaval to which their inhabitants have been exposed. Since images and associations must be useful for both original and new inhabitants, the histories of the immigrants should be interwoven with the history of the new setting. When American families move to a new city, many go out of their way to find houses that in some manner remind them of their childhood homes, even as the Swedish immigrants to the United States looked for "Swedish" landscapes to settle in, and British colonists built British towns. (And thus a native of Calcutta, far from home but new to London, is struck by the nostalgic familiarity of the London scene. He sees the artifacts of home—the mailboxes, railings, details —that the British planners had in their time transplanted to ease their own nostalgia.)

Reference 114

There seems to be some optimum degree of previous development in a changing environment, a degree most satisfactory owing to the low-cost and already depreciated resources that the environment provides, or to the rich variety of facilities and services catering to many preferences that it offers, or to the feeling of being at home that it fosters, or paradoxically, to the way in which it limits and simplifies choice. Yet while too little restraint confuses and impoverishes, too much is costly and frustrating. An environment that cannot be changed invites its own destruction. We prefer a world that can be modified progressively, against a background of valued remains, a world in which one can leave a personal mark alongside the marks of history.

Like law and custom, environment tells us how to act without requiring of us a conscious choice. In a church we are reverent and on a beach relaxed. Much of the time, we are reenacting patterns of behavior associated with particular recognizable settings. A setting may encourage a behavior by its form—a staircase has a shape that is made for going up or down—but also by the expectations associated with it—until recently it was not seemly for adults to sit on stairs. When place changes rapidly, as in a migratory move, people no longer "know how to behave." They must expend effort to test and choose a new form of behavior and to build group agreement. Thus, when change is wanted, a new setting supports the discontinuity. For social continuity it is useful to reenact behavior together in a setting of the past. Claude Lévi-Strauss tells how missionaries were able to disorient the culture of the Bororos by forcing them to abandon the traditional circular layout of their settlements.

Many symbolic and historic locations in a city are rarely visited by its inhabitants, however they may be sought out by tourists. But a threat to destroy these places will evoke a strong reaction, even from those who have never seen, and perhaps never will see, them. The survival of these unvisited, hearsay settings conveys a sense of security and continuity. A portion of the past has been saved as being good, and this promises that the future will so save the present. We have the sense that we and our works will also reach uninterrupted old age. After a catastrophe, the restoration of the symbolic center of community life is a matter of urgency: St. Paul's in burned London, or the "old city" in devastated Warsaw. Symbolic environment is used to create a sense of stability: threatened institutions celebrate their antiquity; kings proclaim their legitimate roots as well as their power. The English gypsies are avid collectors of china and family photographs.

There are striking differences in mood between groups with a valued past, in which they feel rooted, and groups that are living in an isolated present.

Those O'Connells, O'Connors, O'Callaghans, O'Donoghues, were one with the very landscape itself. . . . To run off the family names connected with one of those houses was to call to vision certain districts—hills, rivers and plains; while to recollect the place names in certain regions was to remember the ancient tribes and their memorable deeds. How different it was with the Planters round about them. For them, all that Gaelic background of myth, literature, and history had no existence. . . . The landscape they looked upon was indeed but rocks and stones and trees.

Reference 42

Most Americans still live in secondhand houses, but the homes are not their own. And so they go away from home to Europe to feel at home in time. Their mobility and their lack of attachment to setting were most useful in developing a continent, just as it now serves a role in the rise of Ciudad Guayana. But as tourists in search of cultural roots, Americans inevitably intrude into, and so help to destroy, existing cultured landscapes.

Nietzsche characterizes the settled European as looking on his city and saying, "Here one could live . . . and go on living; for we are tough folk, and will not be uprooted in the night." Harvey Cox tells of a woman from Lidice, the Czech town utterly destroyed and plowed under by the Nazis. She confessed that, despite the loss of her husband and separation from her children, her greatest shock was to come over the crest before Lidice and to find nothing there—not even ruins. Isak Dinesen speaks of the forced relocation of the Masai in East Africa:

Reference 16

Reference 44

The Masai when they were moved from their old country, north of the railway line, to the present reserve, took with them the names of their hills, plains, and rivers, and gave them to the hills, plains, and rivers in the new country. It is a bewildering thing to the traveller. The Masai were carrying their cut roots with them as a medicine.

Reference 48

In the same way, North America is sprinkled with all the place names of Europe.

Quite naturally, there may be sharply divergent historical interests in the same place. The welfare of low-income residents in a "decayed" but historic area can be directly opposed to the desires of members of higher-income groups who do not live there but are aware of its charm and its reference to the past of their kind of people. The wealthy outsiders may hope to occupy and restore the place and

41

may have the resources to do so. If they do, however, historical preservation becomes another cloak for "poor removal," a device to lure the return of the middle class. Restoration is unjust unless present residents can choose to remain in the renewed structures. If they do, renewal is a different affair since existing residents see different values and a different history in the old houses. Frequently, it was *their* ancestors who actually built the fine houses, and in more recent years the history of the place has surely been their own.

Both the temporally rooted and the unrooted are quite different people from those who are reacting against the past, breaking free. The latter are quite conscious of what they are discarding. Symbols of the recent past are sought out and destroyed to clear the way for new behavior. The Paris Commune pulled down the Vendôme Column, a symbol of monarchy.

Reference 106

The Russian Orthodox cathedral in Warsaw was demolished when Poland regained her independence from Russia after World War I. The industrial archaeologist Kenneth Hudson cites a manufacturer who, on assuming command of a family firm, dismantled a historic beam engine to show that he had shaken off his father's rule. The chairman of a gas board destroyed a collection of historic equipment

Reference 63

because it might encourage employees to be "backward-looking." The psychiatrist Rudolf Ekstein described a psychotic child who goes back into the

Reference 50

past with a time machine to "screw it up" and make it more bearable in the present. The great, grim Doric entrance to London's old Euston Station was pulled from its place in front of the characterless modern edifice, not for any compelling technical reason, but because it stood for the old railway age. Preservation is fine for the past that is long past, but yesterday is thought of as something to dump. The head of a firm that was a pioneer in making plastic

Reference 63

products writes in a letter: "I should make it clear that none of the buildings have what can, by any stretch of the imagination, be described as archaeological interest; there is, in fact, nothing earlier than 1923."

The remote past is different, since it does not threaten the present. Abraham Darby's first ironworks at Coalbrookdale have been lovingly restored by Allied Ironfounders. But the works were 250 years old, and the restoration was part of an anniversary celebration. The ironworks no longer were "backward" but had become "historic." The past that is long past may even be cultivated as a justification of the present, as when the French Revolution employed classical symbols.

In opposition to this predilection for the remote past, should we consider establishing a "public attic," where selected old equipment—vehicles, engines, tools, furniture, old clothes, whatever—which was about to be discarded could be available for rummaging? The "attic" would require a continuous maintenance and purging, of course. Reference 116

Might it also be possible to use environment to teach change instead of permanence—how the world constantly shifts in the context of the immediate past; which changes have been valuable, which not; how change can be externally effected; how change ought to occur in the future? Past flux might be communicated by marking out the successive locations of activities or populations or by representing the changing aspect of a single place. The lesson could be disturbing.

Saving the past can be a way of learning for the future, just as people change themselves by learning something now that they may employ later. If advanced education and upward mobility are to be important characteristics of the coming generations, then we might preserve for them a record of the changing educational environment and evidence of the social gaps that had been jumped before. If common ownership of property or an increased sense of public responsibility were desired for the future, then we might save the evidence of past commons. In other situations, we might preserve the corpus of herbal medicine or of technologies suited to more primitive resources or of ways of survival in a hostile environment. Just as we save plant varieties as the raw material of genetic innovation and to avert the disaster of an universal crop failure, so we may wish to save the skills and cultural solutions of the past in order to meet the demands of an uncertain future.

There is a poignancy in evanescence, in something old about to disappear. Old toys, made for brief use, seemingly so fragile, associated with a passing and vulnerable phase of life, are much more emotive symbols than are permanent, serious memorials. In Japan there is an esthetic preference for that which decays and passes. Albert Speer, Hitler's architect, projected himself so far forward into the future as to design his grandiose structures with the hope that they would make noble ruins.

Reference 11

Ruined structures, in the process of going back to the earth, are enjoyed everywhere for the emotional sensations they convey. This pleasurable melancholy may be coupled with the observer's satisfaction at having survived or be tinged with righteous triumph, esthetic delight, or intellectual enjoyment. One may loot the ruin or live in it or put one's name on it. Accumulated literary associations add depth to the experience; place names become pegs for layers of commentaries, as in the Chinese culture. But at base the emotional pleasure is a heightened sense of the flow of time.

Clever restoration obscures the essential quality of impermanent remains. A pleasantly ruinous environment demands some inefficiency, a relaxed acceptance of time, the esthetic ability to take dramatic advantage of destruction. A landscape acquires emotional depth as it accumulates these scars. Certain materials and forms age well. They develop an interesting patina, a rich texture, an attractive outline. Others are at their best only when clean and new; as they grow old, they turn spotted and imperfect.

Archives and Archaeology

Scientific understanding of the past implies archaeological investigation. The aim is analysis, and while fragments may be kept for later study, the process will often destroy the original. Archaeology can be paced to precede new development, and occasionally it is even aided by it. An occupied site contains former buildings and objects, but also crop marks, imprints, traces, foundations, fragments, alterations, significant trash. Most of the information is in the context: how remains relate to each other and to the total setting. Archaeological data are a

Figure 12
Playing with history:
London Bridge, disman-
tled and shipped from the
Thames to the new city of
Lake Havasu in Arizona,
has been reerected with
British flags and an imitation pub. Spanning water
carried from the artificial
lake, it now leads to the
airstrip on the point.

Figure 13
In the immense landscape
of the Mohave Desert, now
invaded by a vast lake, the
new city is a pale scratch-
ing, and London Bridge is a
tiny line of shadow at the
base of the peninsula next
to the temporary airport
road.

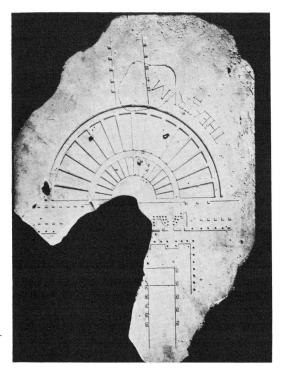

Figure 14
A surviving fragment of
the contemporary marble
map of imperial Rome indicates the theater of
Pompey.

Figure 15
Looking down on the same
area of Rome today, we see
the persistent trace of the
former structure.

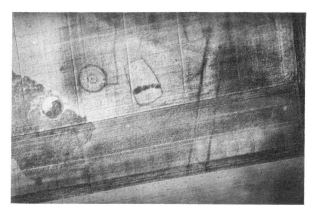

Figure 16
A prehistoric henge leaves
delicate traces on a velvety
British field.

Figure 17
Elsewhere, earth-moving
machinery is erasing old
marks.

Figure 18
A Kwakiutl totem pole
going to decay evokes
strong meanings.

Figure 19
Amateur collectors mine
the California coast for
Indian relics, destroying
the archaeological infor-
mation latent in the site.

nonrenewable resource, convertible to an organized verbal and graphic record but much more easily wasted. Part of the cost of any environmental renewal is therefore a loss of potential information about the past. That cost can be reduced by careful salvage and should at least be accounted for in the balance sheet of any development decision.

The loss of information increases as the rate of development rises, particularly as our technology now encourages us to make massive alterations of the References 39, 46 earth's surface for rural as well as for urban uses. Increasing affluence also spawns antiquarian hobbyists and a brisk market in old artifacts. Sites are churned up; salable items are chopped out, and their context is destroyed. To conserve this information calls for systematic predevelopment salvage, as well as for the preservation of significant areas and contexts for later study, and even the training of amateur hobbyists in the technique of controlled investigations.

Study of the recent past and the workaday world should have an important place in these operations. The rise of industrial archaeology is a hopeful sign. Unfortunately, popular and scientific interests often part company. Many people love old cars and trains, jewelry and palaces. Fewer care for potsherds or early cement mixers or their contexts. But the latter may be more important for understanding the past. Our perceptions guide what we choose to preserve. Old bridges are bold and elegant; they leap up against the force of gravity. Whatever their hidden human costs may have been, they were useful to, and used by, everyone. Old factories, on the other hand, sit heavily on the ground. They were places of noise, stress, and hard labor. They visibly remind us of what it cost this country to achieve its wealth and who paid. Little wonder that few protest the loss of an old factory building.

Since we cannot be certain what will be most relevant in the future, we have an obligation to save some characteristic evidence of every major period—to establish an environmental archive. But an archive, seriously accumulated, will raise all the familiar problems of library management: How is material to be selected? How and when weeded out?

49

How stored? How indexed and arranged for access and retrieval? At what cost? The price of restoration can be substantially larger than the price of building the original object, even in current dollars. We are dealing with buildings and districts that occupy large volumes of space and cannot be left empty, and so the problems of the library are fearfully inflated. The criteria for preservation must be very conservative indeed. Since it is more costly to preserve a whole environment than an object or its representation, there must be a strong reason for doing the former.

The dilemma may justify a monitoring system, which would warn us of the need to consider saving an example of some environmental type as remaining examples of that type became scarce. At least a systematic recording—in words, diagrams, photographs and sound—of typical physical environments and their associated patterns of behavior could be made while they are still flourishing. A recent massive photographic contest in Paris resulted in a recording on film of the look of the entire city, by small zones 250 meters square. What an archive for the future, particularly if done recurrently and if attentive to human behavior as well as to physical setting!

In addition, it may become necessary to create a procedure for notifying interested public and private agencies of the intent to demolish and of the nature of the environment that will thereby be erased, as is now being done in certain designated districts of New York City. This approach goes as far beyond the present demolition license as the contemporary building permit (with its specification of the intended structure, use, location, appearance, and supporting services) goes beyond earlier regulations. Licensing demolition would provide an occasional opportunity for acquisition to preserve but more often for predevelopment salvage or recording or for a chance to encourage a creative remodeling of the old premises. There should therefore be agencies concerned with recording, listing, and, if necessary, saving representative living environments.

No such comprehensive approach to the recording and conservation of the valued environmental past has yet been made. The Landmark Commission of the city of New York is perhaps the most advanced historical preservation agency in the United States, and it is no more than on the way toward exercising a comprehensive preservation policy. It now has 320 landmarks and 14 districts containing 5000 buildings under its control. Intermittently, once every three years, it has the power to designate landmarks or preservation districts. Once designated, the exterior form of a landmark or a building in such a district may not be modified without a certificate from the commission, nor may it be demolished until after a year's delay, during which time the commission may seek a buyer or user who will keep the exterior intact. The administrative load on the commission is understandably heavy.

But the decision to designate a building or site is based primarily on the special architectural quality of the structure or area and secondarily on its historic interest. The commission is more concerned about preserving and developing worthwhile present character than about restoring the aspect of a historic period. The commission looks for a local constituency to support the preservation and is therefore most successful in settled middle-class residential communities with active neighborhood organizations. It is empowered to adjust the building and zoning codes in special cases and to propose more general changes where impending new development could usefully be guided.

Activities as well as structures are preserved. Loss of the city's unique theater district, for example, was averted by encouragement of the building of new theaters. New control devices such as zoning bonuses, scenic easements, compacts between owners, or transferable development rights are tried out. The management, financing, and marketing of historic structures are studied as closely as is their physical condition. New uses for old buildings are actively sought. While controlling over 5000 buildings, the commission has been taken to court in only six cases.

Historical knowledge must be communicated to the public for its enjoyment and education. Words and pictures convey much, but real things make the

Communicating the Past

51

deepest impression. It is a sign of the verbal dominance of our civilization that we call any period without written documents "prehistoric." To be surrounded by the buildings and equipment of the past, or best of all to act as if we were in the past, is an excellent way to learn about it. The creation of skillful illusion requires one to move and concentrate structures and equipment or to counterfeit them. This ambience can then be peopled with live actors.

There are more than 125 museum villages and extensive city walking tours in the United States today, in forty-two of the fifty states. They re-create some particular period with the buildings and equipment of the time, often with simulated inhabitants who dress and act—even think—their parts. These reconstructions are tremendously popular. But they suffer some necessary limitations beyond cost, or information, or the availability of old artifacts, or accuracy in the light of changing scholarship. There can be problems of comfort (heavy wool clothes in the summer, for example, or the stink of indigo curing), or of social sanction (low-cut dresses, or the growing of hemp), or health and safety (dangerous tools and unsanitary conditions), or of isolation from what had been a total social and geographic system, or of the unwillingness or inability of present-day actors to take historic roles. There are modern myths to avoid, or temptations to sugarcoat the past, to forget the caste rigidity and social isolation of a military post, for example. How can children be induced to play the way they used to? Who wants to demonstrate a shameful or unwanted past, particularly if the show is for some presumably "superior" group of spectators? The villagers of delightfully retarded Stensjö, put on the national payroll when it became a Swedish historic area, soon wanted to enjoy modern facilities, and, when rebuffed, they simply moved away. Reconstructed environments exist today and not in the past time they mimic, and they are filled with modern tourists.

Passive demonstrations are the rule: the visitors gape and move on. Such enterprises would be even more effective if the observers were instructed to become the actors. The ordinary equipment of the time should be available for use. However clumsily, visitors might smooth with an adz, wear old clothes, cook and eat according to old recipes, dance the quadrille, plow with oxen, or warp a yardarm around. In that way they might begin to penetrate into some sense of the life of an earlier time. Were the visitors given the opportunity to live for a week as the people of that time lived and to suffer, at least temporarily, some of the real pleasures and penalties of adequate performance, the penetration would be deeper. A small group of high school students recently spent five days in a one-room cottage in the reconstructed Plimoth Plantation in Massachusetts. Reference 89 They wore heavy Pilgrim clothes, ate the coarse Pilgrim food, cooked it over an open fire, hauled wood and water, scoured pots with sand, read and sewed by firelight. It was a difficult but instructive week. Even then, they knew they were not threatened by starvation, disease, or Indian attack.

The settings should illustrate not simply the "great" moments of the period but the full spectrum of its culture. Re-created pasts ought to be based on the knowledge and values of the present. We want them to change as present knowledge and values change, just as history is rewritten. One danger in the preservation of environment lies in its very power to encapsulate some image of the past, an image that may in time prove to be mythical or irrelevant. For preservation is not simply the saving of old things but the maintaining of a response to those things. This response can be transmitted, lost, or modified. It may survive beyond the real thing itself. We should expect to see conflicting views of the past, based on the conflicting values of the present. Diverse environmental museums might present divergent interpretations of the Civil War, for example, or the Yankee and Irish views of what it was like in Boston in the 1850s. They would look at the conquest of the West through Indian eyes as well as those of the white pioneer. If so, it should be possible for a student to go from one presentation to the other, in the same way that he can compare different verbal interpretations. Environmental preservation has always had political as well as esthetic and educational motives. Groups in power save prominent symbols of their prestige, while others must be more discreet. But plural meanings could be made explicit in reconstruction.

The city itself can be a historical teaching device, an aim now served by the occasional guided tour or plaque. That "William Blake lived here" is trivial, unless the visible structure influenced what Blake did, or expressed his personality, or unless its location had some bearing on his personal history. The city can be enormously informative, since the pattern of remains is a vast if jumbled historical index. Signs, tours, guides, and other communications devices can bring out the latent history of a complex site, with little of the interference with present function that may be caused by massive physical reconstructions. The kingly bypass of a rebellious City of London by the water route from Westminster to the Tower can be demonstrated, or the successive flights of middle-class residents before the oncoming workingmen. Illustrated walks can be laid out, and crucial remains made visible—incorporated in other structures or underground or even underwater. The past can be shown in immediate relevance to the present: old-fashioned clothes in a clothing store, former work methods in a factory, previous illustrations of a site on the site itself. Indeed, the resources going into communication should be as large as, or larger than, those devoted to preservation.

The image of the physical environment has been used for centuries as a mental peg on which to hang material to be remembered, from the memory system of Simonides of Ceos in 500 B.C. to the imaginary walks of S. V. Shereshevskii in this century. In the sixteenth century, Camillo actually built a memory theater in Venice, a wooden structure whose seats, gangways, and images had the sole purpose of symbolizing man's knowledge of the universe. Martin Pawley has recently suggested a "time house"—a family dwelling unit that automatically records and on request replays the sights and sounds of the life of the house. The thought that family life would be continuously watched and recorded is a little chilling, but it is quite reasonable to think that the real remains of a city, in conjunction with print, film, and recording, might consciously be used to retain and teach what we think to be instructive for

Reference 112

the future. Could mute statues, for example, be associated with explanatory recordings or photographs that were available on request? Tommaso Campanella proposed that the walls of his utopia would illustrate the knowledge of history and the natural world. In a similar way the cathedrals vividly presented the Christian dogmas to the faithful.

Even now, environment interacts with other memory systems—with books and tales and film. Thus for an American in London for the first time but brought up on English children's stories, the names of streets and places are unsettlingly familiar. In the opposite case, a man-made environment may become completely detached from its previous meanings. For the medieval village that reoccupied it, the abandoned Diocletian palace at Spalato (the modern Split) must have simply been a natural landscape to be overcome. And furthermore quite false meanings may be attached to a place. So tourists enjoy the absurd but colorful tales that their guides fasten to the passing scene. The children of Manhattan, Kansas, now tell their own stories about the statue of Johnny Kaw, a "folk hero" hurriedly invented by the city fathers for a centennial celebration and as quickly forgotten by the elders. False history, which leads blacks to wear dashikis or former forest Indians to live in tipis—is also a means of mobilizing people to meet problems of today.

Thus there is something to say about archives, **Present Value** about the creation of special teaching areas, and about the uses of communication to teach environmental history. What can be said about preservation in extensive inhabited regions? Here the aim should be the conservation of present value as well as the maintenance of a sense of near continuity. Things are useful to us for their actual current qualities and not for some mystic essence of time gone by. We should save old houses if we cannot replace the equivalent space at a lower cost (recognizing that a possible increased consumption of natural resources in new building as compared with rehabilitation is a real, though often hidden, cost) or if we simply cannot reproduce valuable features of form or equipment. Often enough, old environment is worth conserving because it is completely amortized, or was built by cheap skilled labor or with materials now unobtainable, or was constructed to high standards for the affluent but was abandoned by them. Moreover, it may be a specially valuable artistic creation difficult to imitate or may be part of a whole network of facilities and social connections that we cannot easily reconstruct. Taking rational account of existing values should not be clouded by dogma about the intrinsic goodness of old things. The most famous artists of the day protested vehemently against the erection of the Eiffel Tower. Cultures that produced fine environment were confident of their ability to create afresh, and we may notice in this connection the disdain for preservation, even of their own works, that is found among many creative artists.

If old environments are superior to new ones (sometimes they are, sometimes not), then we must study them to see what these superior qualities are, so that we can achieve them in a new way. Old buildings, even quite unremarkable ones, often have certain advantages over new structures, along with their typical disadvantages of poor utilities, an unsafe framework, a cramped floor plan, or expensive maintenance. They are likely to have a richer form, with the impress of many occupants, a well-adjusted fit between activity and form, a luxurious "wastefulness" of odd pieces of space, a more intimate scale, mellowed surfaces, and detail. Many of these qualities are reproducible in new construction, although at a cost of money and design attention. In regulating the replacement of older areas, the focus should be on identifying the present values in existing buildings and on insisting that new development equal or better those qualities before it is permitted to occur.

Present value will be particular to a certain group of people. Such a group is the necessary political base for restoration work. Areas that do not have a resident constituency—a partly abandoned nineteenth-century commercial district, for example —will be the most difficult to save. Then it is necessary to organize a nonresident base that is touristic or region-wide. Or the planner must be able to teach others to see the present values of an area, or, even harder, to persuade them that in another generation they will be valued.

When present value is not obvious, a careful analysis may be required to disentangle the valued qualities. For example, what and for whom are the present values of an existing slum environment, whose arrangements may support, but also enforce, a certain way of life? In Bath, as a contrasting example, a landscape analysis would reveal those qualities of space, scale, and facade texture that, if also achieved in new structures, would allow the replacement of many areas of the town which serve as a visual background for the more noteworthy structures and would do so without imitation and without loss. Historical areas are not so much irreplaceable as rarely replaced.

Where old structures cannot support present functions without impairing those functions, and unless they are of exceptional didactic or esthetic value, they can be cleared away, although their fragments may be used to enhance new buildings. We need not be so concerned about perfect conformity to past form but ought rather to seek to use remains to enhance the complexity and significance of the present scene. The contrast of old and new, the accumulated concentration of the most significant elements of the various periods gone by, even if they are only fragmentary reminders of them, will in time produce a landscape whose depth no one period can equal, although such time-deep areas may be achieved only in some parts of the city. The esthetic aim is to heighten contrast and complexity, to make visible the process of change. The achievement of the aim requires creative and skillful demolition, just as much as skillful new design.

We look for a setting that, rather than simply being a facsimile of the past, seems to open outward in time. To quote Vladimir Nabokov, in his description of his years in Cambridge, England:

Fragmentary Reminders

Nothing one looked at was shut off in terms of time, everything was a natural opening into it, so that one's mind grew accustomed to work in a particularly pure and ample environment, and because, in terms of space, the narrow lane, the cloistered lawn,

Reference 15

Figure 20
Inca masonry lines the
streets of Cuzco in Peru,
still carrying the modern
structures above, still pro-
claiming the Inca past.

Figure 21
The first Neolithic man
found preserved in a
Danish bog. We feel the
shock of a short circuit of
time.

Figure 22
Old chairs arranged for a
Shaker meeting between
men and women. Ghosts
occupy them. We have an
intuition of that utopian
society.

the dark archway hampered one physically, that yielding diaphanous texture of time was, by contrast, especially welcome to the mind, just as a sea view from a window exhilarates one hugely, even though one does not care for sailing.

Our new suburbs and new towns, on the other hand, seem all begun yesterday and completely finished then. There is no crevice through which one can venture back or forward.

We could enjoy these qualities even in the most ordinary areas, where there may be little of real distinction to be saved. Everywhere, even in regions to be swept clean for rebuilding, we can retain some environmental memories that go back at least to the first reminiscences of the living generation, say for sixty years. But since the generations overlap endlessly, and since current needs may require more or less demolition in any small region, it will be impossible to preserve a whole context. We then resort to saving symbols and fragments of a demolished environment, embedded in the new context for another generation.

Saved elements could be of many kinds, though they should not be random or trivial. Haphazard exhibits will create a sense of the past as chaos. Where possible, it is best to save something indicative of the old ambience: its scale, its spaces or pathways, its plantings. Where this is not possible, it is desirable to seek to keep things of high symbolic meaning or things that were directly connected with the actions of remembered people: crosses, seats, steps. But what is saved must be based on what users wish to remember or can connect with themselves. The implication is that the planner will seek to learn what inhabitants remember and wish to remember. Furthermore, since new urban development is almost always somehow constrained by previous patterns, we ought to make clear this influence of the past, marking the history of an environment on itself. Such patterns can be woven into a new design with little of the difficulty ordinarily associated with area-wide preservation. They could be part of our habitual concern for the character of a site.

Personal Connection

If we examine the feelings that accompany daily life, we find that historic monuments occupy a small place. Our strongest emotions concern our own lives and the lives of our family or friends because we have known them personally. The crucial reminders of the past are therefore those connected with our own childhood, or with our parents' or perhaps our grandparents' lives. Remarkable things are directly associated with memorable events in those lives: births, deaths, marriages, partings, graduations. To live in the same surroundings that one recalls from earliest memories is a satisfaction denied to most Americans today. The continuity of kin lacks a corresponding continuity of place. We are interested in a street on which our father may have lived as a boy; it helps to explain him to us and strengthens our own sense of identity. But our grandfather or great-grandfather, whom we never knew, is already in the remote past; his house is "historical."

Most historical preservation, focused as it is on the classic past, moves people only momentarily, at a point remote from their vital concerns. It is impersonal as well as ancient. Near continuity is emotionally more important than remote time, although the distant past may seem nobler, more mysterious or intriguing to us. There is a spatial simile: feeling locally connected where we customarily range is more important than our position at a national scale, although occasional realization of the latter can impart a brief thrill. In this sense, we should seek to preserve the near and middle past, the past with which we have real ties. The family photograph or the heap of flowers in Dallas is a strong thing.

It is the signs of the near past which we connect with our own continuity as a living person:

Over the ground from which all vestiges of the past had been taken away, he walked like a man lost. . . . "But when did it all go?" He was shocked to see how a place too could change. . . . People didn't really change very much, he thought, they only decayed. They were not like this place, which had not only changed beyond recognition, but gained new vigor in the process. As the contrast struck him he could not help wondering: "And what about me? What will I be like in the end?"

Reference 95

A humane environment commemorates recent events quickly and allows people to mark out their own growth. It is more human not only for the inhabitant but for the observer as well. He will sense its warmth and find in it a symbolic way of meeting its inhabitants. But there must also be some means of removing these marks as they recede in time or lose connections with present persons. This is forgetting again. There is a pleasure in seeing receding, half-veiled space or in detecting the various layers of successive occupation as they fade into the past—and then in finding a few fragments whose origins are remote and inscrutable, whose meanings lurk beneath their shapes, like dim fish in deep water. We do not wish to preserve our childhood intact, with all its personalities, circumstances, and emotions. We want to simplify and to pattern it, to make vivid its important moments, to skip over its empty stretches, sense its mysterious beginnings, soften its painful feelings—that is, to change it into a dramatic recital.

Nabokov, in his *Speak, Memory*, gives us a moving and beautiful memory of his childhood and adolescence in Russia. Time is compressed and expanded, folded in on itself. His patient evocation of the dog on the beach of childhood and the protracted search for her name locks suddenly into his memory of the view forward to a distant cloudscape seen far beyond a chaotic sunset. He enters a Russian bog in 1910, hunting butterflies, and emerges years later near Long's Peak in Colorado.

Reference 15

I confess I do not believe in time. I like to fold my magic carpet, after use, in such a way as to superimpose one part of the pattern on another. Let visitors trip. And the highest enjoyment of timelessness is when I stand among rare butterflies. . . . This is ecstasy . . . like a momentary vacuum into which rushes all that I love. A sense of oneness . . .

Personal connection is most effectively made by personal imprints on the environment. New customs might connect environment symbolically to personal experience. The stages of physical growth can be imprinted on our surroundings by height marks, foot or hand prints. Portraits and photographs may be mounted to give a place a visible genealogy. We are accustomed to marking death with a stone; can we also so signify birth? We could plant a tree in a community grove, a tree that gradually merges into the forest. Memorials may refer to a family or an individual or an age group: a gang or a school grade. Stones and trees may be carried with us when we move, to make a personal link to a new landscape, just as we bring familiar furniture with us to personalize our new interiors. Old inhabitants should be encouraged to record their memories of a place. The recording could then be made available nearby, in a branch library or a street information center. As in some primitive societies, burial might at first be in some nearby and conspicuous location, later removed to a marked place in a community site and, much later, when living kin are gone, to a common unmarked grave. Our distant and crowded cemeteries are devices for sealing away the dead from the living under the fiction of eternal remembrance.

There can be temporary memorials for recent events, to be replaced later by permanent markings, if the event remains memorable. Our cities are mute about the persons for whom we care but littered with statues to generals and statesmen now in limbo. When 370 Liverpudlians were asked about the public statuary of their city, one-quarter of them had no picture of the large concentration of sculpture outside St. George's Hall, and most of the rest were confused about who was commemorated there, although many remembered the lions. One-half of the residents ignored the figures above the Mersey Tunnel entrance, under which 22,000 cars pass daily.

Reference 109

Though the landscape should have the imprint of human events and seem connected with living persons, the imprints and connections must eventually fade away and be forgotten, just as human memories and generations fade. The old men of the Isleta Reservation retell the ancient stories but will not write them down. "When the stories are no longer told, there will no longer be a need for them."

Thus I propose a plural attitude toward environmental remains, depending on the particular motive. Where it is scientific study, there would be dissection, recording, and scholarly storage; where it is education, I propose unabashed playacting and communication; where it is the enhancement of present value and a sense of the flow of time, I should encourage temporal collage, creative demolition and addition; where it is personal connection, I suggest making and retaining imprints as selective and impermanent as memory itself. To preserve effectively, we must know for what the past is being retained and for whom. The management of change and the active use of remains for present and future purpose are preferable to an inflexible reverence for a sacrosanct past. The past must be chosen and changed, made in the present. Choosing a past helps us to construct a future.

Alive Now

3

To begin with historical preservation is traditional. It must seem evident to anyone that the serious issues of environment revolve about either the preservation of the past or the control of the future. But that is wrong. We preserve present signals of the past or control the present to satisfy our images of the future. Our images of past and future are present images, continuously re-created. The heart of our sense of time is the sense of "now." The spatial environment can strengthen and humanize this present image of time, and I contend that this function is one of its vital but most widely neglected roles. In a sense, then, I began at the wrong point and must begin again.

We have two kinds of evidence of the passage of time. One is rhythmic repetition—the heartbeat, breathing, sleeping and waking, hunger, the cycles of sun and moon, the seasons, waves, tides, clocks. The other is progressive and irreversible change—growth and decay, not recurrence but alteration. Men have made magical attempts to see the second phenomenon as a cosmic variant of the first, to pretend that change is also cyclical, to imagine that progressive time is a series of eternal, contrasting repetitions, each arising from the other. That magic warms the spirit with the sense that decline and dissolution are only appearances, that resurrection will follow. But the things we love do not in fact come back to us. Whatever our hopes, we know things change.

We are aware that the time inside is different from the time outside. Social time, which coordinates the actions of many people, may not match the internal rhythms of the body. The precise, abstract time of science and efficiency is certainly far removed from that inner experience. Individuals caught between cycle and flow, between subjective and "objective" time, may try to suppress one or the other. They will schedule their lives very precisely and in great detail, or they will insulate themselves from objective time by keeping ostentatiously erratic hours, by willful disorganization, by stupor. They attend entertainments to forget time, or to "kill" it.

Reference 54
When a prisoner is condemned to die all clocks in the neighborhood of the death cell are stopped; as if the removal of the clock will cut off the flow of time and maroon the prisoner on a coast of timelessness where the moments, like breakers, rise and surge near but never touch the shore. But . . . in the death cell time flows in as if all the cuckoo clocks grandfather clocks alarm clocks were striking simultaneously. . . .

Men have always been concerned with *timing*, however little or much they may care about the distant past or future. They are necessarily preoccupied with the practical problems of allocating time, of coordinating joint activities. But beyond that they attempt to harmonize their perceptions of inner and outer time, to feel the fullness of life, and to still the anxiety of death. If this is the aim, then environment ought to support it. Environment is the clock we read to tell real time, to tell personal time.

Telling Time

Most adults in the "advanced" countries carry a watch. We depend on it, and it makes us uneasy. We eat and sleep and work as the watch may indicate, suppressing internal signals. When "time" or schedule changes, we jump to follow. To be asked the hour is a common street question, for in a scheduled society objective time is critical information. We repeatedly check our mental sense of objective time with external clues and may be quite upset when inner time and external clues are contradictory. Is our watch wrong, or are we ill? Journeys in modern cities are measured as time consumed and are accompanied by calculations of how late or early it is acceptable to be at journey's end. The city is a medium through which we make our way by spending time. We "waste" time or sometimes "gain" it. Refusing to carry a watch or to be bound by normal schedules is one way of declaring independence from conventional society.

Telling time is a simple technical problem, but unfortunately the clock is a rather obscure perceptual device. Its first widespread use in the thirteenth century was to ring the hours for clerical devotions. The clockface, which translated time into spatial alteration, came later. That form was dictated by its works, not by any principle of perception. Two (sometimes three) superimposed cycles give duplicate readings, according to angular displacement around a finely marked rim. Neither minutes nor hours nor half days correspond to the natural cycles of our bodies or the sun. And so teaching a child to read a clock is not a childish undertaking. When asked why a clock had two hands, a four-year-old replied, "God thought it would be a good idea." Reference 17

Take another example. A traffic signal, which also measures time, is a visually sudden event, a featureless duration, whose abrupt transformation is tensely awaited. Other external time signals in normal use are equally unfitted to human perception. Electric bells and buzzers regulate the scheduling of schools, factories, and other prisons, just as bells were used to order life in the monastery. These aural signals are sudden and intrusive: the listener has no warning of their coming, yet he must attend to them. But as an occasional event, the noon gun or siren and the evening peal—particularly when they do not constrain us to instant action—make a cheerful sound, simply reminding us of common time. And many unintentional sounds also tell time: the hum of traffic swells and wanes, birds greet the sun, a scheduled train passes. Someone remembers, as a child on a hill, hearing the city "sit down" to its noonday meal, when doors slammed and then everything was quiet.

Occasionally an observer wants precise readings. Digital clocks display precise time, but they give us little sense of time structure or movement. Better, the ball topping the Greenwich tower rises slowly, then drops just at noon, to give exact observatory time to the ships in the river.

Often, we want environmental signals that are nonintrusive, that take on identifiable forms at significant times of the day (noon, closing hours) after giving us a progressive warning of the transformation to come and express the general passage of time by some gradual background change. The wasting sand in the hourglass is a vivid perceptual device, though of brief duration. The sun fits our prescription, particularly at its rising and setting, but sun angle is a mystery to most city people. Sundials clarify the ambiguities of sun position and can be dramatic at a large scale. The moon is even more vivid,

Figure 23
The time ball atop the old
Royal Observatory, Green-
wich, England. First lifted
slowly on its pole, it was
then dropped precisely
at noon to give exact time
to the ships in the river
below. The roof in the left
foreground defines Lon-
gitude 0°, the Greenwich
Meridian.

since it changes its shape every night, but its cycle has less relevance for us and its hourly position requires sophisticated observation.

We might prefer to have time signals that, while giving us the information we need to make social coordination possible, also fit natural cycles and our inner sense of time and are clearly suited to our ways of sensing things. Thus it is amusing to think of clocks that might go by five-minute leaps. Or ones that would pass more rapidly through the hour than the points of hourly transition or use other units of time that better approximate our normal spans of attention and effort than does the hour. For another reason than the one we have in mind, nineteenth-century factory managers sometimes used clocks that moved faster during the lunch period. Perhaps we could devise other time signals: pointers moving along a linear scale, forms that change their orientation progressively and take on special characteristics at key times, lights that move like suns. We still enjoy the fabulous mechanical displays of the great public clocks of the late Middle Ages. Scented candles in Japanese temples emitted a different odor for each period of time. If the clear signaling of objective time is a modern requirement, fitting those signals to our rhythms and to our modes of perception is a more pervasive human one.

As we spend more of our lives in interior environments, we are deprived of many natural clues to the passage of day and season. Office and factory buildings, long corridors, and subways are timeless environments, like caves or the deep sea. Light, climate, and visible form are invariant. Without external oscillations to keep our rhythms in phase, our schedules may become erratic. Emerging, we enter with a shock into heat or darkness. As technical advances separate us from these natural clues, we may be forced to some ingenious simulations. The imitation window, with its curtains, painted view, and eternal yellow light, is merely depressing. A radio or television broadcast of external conditions is somewhat better. Light, heat, or sound, or even visible surfaces that change in congruence with the daily cycles may be acceptable signs of time. They could occur in corridors and lobbies, which would then become the "outside" of these artificial worlds. Where separation from the normal rhythm is prolonged, these artificial settings may occasionally even be used to modify time, by changing its cycle or rate.

More direct and satisfying, where we can use them, are the arrangements that amplify or complement the underlying natural clues of time: surfaces that catch the light and change character as the sun angle shifts, plants that transform themselves with the seasons. Exterior light or heat may be complementary to or in contrast with natural change: the pool of warmth on an icy day, reddish lights that magnify the sunset, streetlights that dim with the passage of the night (or perhaps even change with phases of the moon?). One of the great values of the city park or garden is the way in which its plants and surfaces convey the passage of the year. Its leaves rustle, or its mantle of snow muffles sound. But the natural clues often fail us—a gray sky covers the sun, or an English spring may be too "slow" for one accustomed to more dramatic seasons. Nor are our clues solely natural ones—great cities have rhythms of sound, light, and visible activity which convey time and season to the experienced observer as vividly as does the sun. These clues might also be amplified and sharpened.

Reading the time of day or year is only part of the information we require. We want to coordinate our activity with the activities of others, and objective time is only a means for doing this. Knowing whether a store is open now or how long it will be before we meet someone or when a train leaves is the information we are after. We use printed schedules and appointment books and compare them with our watches, but visible clues are more reassuring: Is the train actually in the station now? Are people at the theater door? Is his car outside? Can you see the bus yet? A satisfying public environment not only will display the general time of day in some humane and vivid way and give precise time on call but will also indicate the timing of publicly accessible activities: the opening of stores or restaurants, the presence of trains and audiences, the occurrence of the rush hour.

Even more than current timing, we are eager to know predicted timing: When will this restaurant close? Is the train coming soon? Will the parking lot be full when I arrive? When *will* the parade begin? Experienced city observers use subtle clues to extract this information, or depend on long experience, or refer to terse announcements. We are accustomed to nervous waiting and repeated questions, since the information must be had time and again. An environment that displayed those facts clearly and from a distance would be more comforting. Could bus stops tell us how many minutes away the bus is, or could highway signs display the predicted hours of congestion for that day?

Different observers in different situations have diverse needs for time information, some urgent, some casual. Tourists and strangers, for example, have pressing requirements for what may seem to others to be obvious information about the timing of activities. Just as we are beginning to study the locational information needed by different people, so should we be learning what they want to know about the timing of city events and how they use the perception of time in everyday life.

We might establish a public temporal (and spatial) model of the city to include short-term fluctuations such as the timing of events and the current loads on the communications systems, as well as long-term changes like past, present, and near-future shifts in population or the housing stock, in addition to the spatial locations of persons, activities, and facilities. This store of temporal and spatial information would respond to particular inquiries by presenting changing maps and models, slides, movies, graphic computer outputs, or tabulations of specific data. Schoolchildren might use it, as well as tourists, private researchers, official agencies, or people looking for a house, for a commercial site, for a job, for entertainment, for medical aid, for some social service. This picture of "what's happening" in the city could be scanned at will or searched in depth at chosen points. I am suggesting a public war room, used for peaceful purposes. This is Patrick Geddes's old idea in modern form. A modest and temporary prototype has already been tried with great success in Boston.

Reference 24

Until recently environmental design was preoccupied with the permanent physical artifacts: buildings, roads, and land. But the human activities occurring among those artifacts are of equal or greater importance to the quality of a place. With this principle in mind, physical design has been broadened to become spatial design, planning the form of behavior and things in space. But if it is to deal with behavior, it must consider the temporal as well as the spatial pattern, and it becomes an art of managing the changing form of objects and the standing patterns of human activity in space and time together. Activities shift cyclically and progressively within their relatively unchanging spatial containers. The form of those containers cannot therefore "follow function" unless the use of a space is reduced to some single, invariant type of behavior. And allocating spaces to a single use (which seems to be an increasing tendency today) is usually inefficient and often socially isolating. The timing of an action or a physical intervention has as much to do with the good functioning and style of a place as does the location of that action or intervention.

Generally, timing is still casually dealt with. Plans and proposals rarely refer to desired or expected timing, except in reference to the peak loads on transportation channels. Activity timing is fixed by custom. In principle it can be manipulated more freely than activity location, yet in fact it is so far less amenable to rational control. The individual, although he has some freedom of maneuver, is still meshed in an interlocking pattern of accepted timings—of hours for meals, for work, for travel, for play, for sleep. Problems of congestion and scarcity arise not solely because many want the same things but because they want the same things at the same time.

The allocation of time becomes a problem as we begin to see that we may have some choice in the matter. Leisure is now possible for many, and customs of timing are more obvious and less absolute.

Time has become both more valuable and also more subject to reallocation. An art of choosing and distributing time has to be learned.

To begin with an obvious issue, environmental design must at least take careful account of when things are likely to happen in order to size and locate the spatial facilities properly. Thus there must be an accepted way of representing and quantifying activity sequences, so that a proposed environment can be seen and judged as a spatiotemporal whole.

Occasionally, we may also seek to control or influence the timing of events, as part of a planned proposal. The critical points are the beginnings and endings of coherent streams, or packages, of behavior: sleeping, eating together, playing a game, buying groceries. We need some guide as to what makes one pattern better in timing than another.

The most familiar case of the control of timing is the scheduling of the building process, in which the aim is to avoid bottlenecks, coordinate complementary operations, make efficient use of resources, and maintain a general sequence. But we also schedule the use of scarce space, such as a concert hall, or regulate the timing of public services, such as transit, and thus affect the timing of many other activities as a secondary consequence. We may set temporal limits to certain behavior, as by blue laws or closing hours. We may try to spread a load by lowering prices or raising attractiveness in off-hours, or by compelling a staggered use. Alternatively, in the case of a specialized activity, we peak its load more sharply at some particular time so as to generate sufficient demand (market days are an example). An agency may fix some key time for a special event: a holiday, a meeting, a celebration. And it is conceivable that an institution or public body might initiate a new timing pattern by introducing a service or activity at some unusual hour.

Some of these motives for interfering with timing, or at least for taking account of it, are well known. We may seek to fit load to capacity. We may try to fit complementary activities together in time or to separate those that conflict, as when we restrict truck loadings to the night hours. We put actions into a proper sequence so that none is held up for want of an adequate antecedent—this is the meat of most scheduling studies. Or we may be concerned with allocation, with seeing that each activity has enough time, that it has the right kind of time for its purpose, and that an interrelated set of activities does not take up more than a given total extent of time (as a daily cycle or an allowable construction period). This will involve the adjustments of conflicts between competing time demands.

These motives of activity coordination, of load adjustment, and of time allocation have their counterparts in the manipulation of spatial patterns, of course. Other motives now not so familiar may be just as important, however. As we learn more about the inherent rhythms of the body (sleep, excretion, eating, attention, mood), we may find that we should rearrange established timings to achieve a better fit: hours of work, study, and rest, the availability of meals, the pattern of journeys, and many other activities the environment must be designed and timed to support. Eventually, we may even decide to readjust certain artificial time divisions, for instance, hours and weeks. While many of these possibilities lie in a future in which we hope to have more certain knowledge, there are functions that may today be ripe for temporal modification. The timing of meals and of classes in school and the use of rotating shifts in business and industry come to mind. Temporal modifications will often have spatial consequences, as in the location of rest rooms.

In addition to adjusting time to conform to bodily rhythms, we can interfere with timing in order to increase choice and diversity and thus to allow individuals to package their days in ways better suited to their constitutions or their situations. Basic services and facilities could be made more widely available in time as well as in space. Fewer restrictions could be put on the temporal location of activity. Shops need not be forced to close on Sundays, or pubs in the afternoon. Time patterns rooted in history survive their functions, like vermiform appendixes. Attempts can be made to loosen the hold of custom or the tyranny of a tight intermeshing of behavior. Most schools, for example, still insist that everyone learn the same material at the same pace in the same block of time. A few have demonstrated that this absolutism is unnecessary. Some office work can now occur at unconventional times, and an occasional business enterprise will allow individual workers to set the hours to which they wish to be held. Thus one of the satisfactions enjoyed by artists and independent craftsmen can be transferred into large commercial firms.

Finally, it is conceivable that one might try to manipulate activity timing to enhance the sequential character of a place or of a person's day. Summer camps, for example, begin the day with calisthenics and end it with singing. A desirable character, in this sense, implies that a day or a locality should have a perceptible rhythm of events, memorable peaks and moments of calm, behavior sometimes synchronized, sometimes free and easy. This is a peculiar, interesting, and rather dangerous idea. The possible characteristics of some sequences will be the subject of discussion to come but will be treated with caution. We should be fearful of ordering the timing of a person's day directly, except where that ordering is unavoidable for necessary economic or social functions or contains a sufficient number of alternatives. Imposed timing—the curfew, for example—is a technique of domination.

The timing of behavior has always been a strong expression of group or personal style. There are morning people and evening people, those who linger over a late social dinner and those who eat alone whenever hungry. Some move easily through the day, coordinating with others only when necessary. Others are harried—bound to iron schedules and yet never on time. The questions are not only how people actually organize their time but also how they would prefer to organize it and how they would respond to new time organizations they have never tried before. Schools are experimenting with flexible schedules in which pupils work at tasks according to the demands of the work itself and not within conventional blocks of time. Individuals should be given both the opportunity and the knowledge to create their own time order. They should be encouraged to learn the time structure of their own bodies, and to search for a timing of behavior that is in tune with it.

Increasing the range of timing choices is valuable but not by itself sufficient. A good pattern is one that is stable and coherent, that is shared by others, and that fits external rhythms and requirements and also the internal structure of the individual. It is not a casual creation. Ideally, perhaps, within the limits of necessary large-scale social coordination, timing patterns would be the product of the trials and experiences of small groups who are of like mind and in similar circumstances. The flair for timing one's actions with grace and skill may be taught as well as enjoyed. At any rate, we could illustrate some of the possibilities in addition to allowing a greater choice.

Packaging Time

We could make a fantasy about a world in which external time were paced to fit subjective time, as it is in wishes, memory, and dreams— where events speeded up or slowed down as desired. Moments of pleasure might be stretched out, pain raced through, sleep brief, and waking long. But as a result, social coordination would collapse. The individual would be stripped of temporal clues, except those which reflected his own internal feelings. Personal worlds could race to a blowup or run down to stasis. Studies of behavior in the isolation of caves and the Antarctic have revealed the instabilities, distortions, and difficulties of an externally timeless environment. Our pleasant fantasy becomes a nightmare. We do manipulate time when we indulge in reverie. But the external social world must be attended to recurrently and must have a stable time structure. Moreover, our society is a highly programmed one. The clock is ubiquitous; sometimes even minimum speeds are fixed.

One can think of several dimensions along which time structure can vary:

(a) its grain, or the size and precision of the chunks into which it is divided;

(b) its period, or the length of time within which events recur;

(c) its amplitude, or the degree of change within a cycle;

(d) its rate, or the speed with which changes occur;

(e) its synchronization, or the degree to which the cycles and changes are in phase, or begin and end together;

(f) its regularity, or the degree to which the preceding characteristics themselves remain stable and unchanging, and

(g) (in the human case and more subjectively) its orientation, or the degree to which attention is focused on past, present, or future.

We are accustomed to thinking of these dimensions as being strictly bound together. We feel that a fine-grained, short-period, ample, rapid, synchronized, regular, near-future-oriented time structure is a "natural" (and perhaps unpleasant but inevitable) combination. Yet other structures are possible and may have advantages. For example, a coarse-grained yet synchronized time framework might be workable. Might a diversity of time structures better fit individual needs and the requirements of different kinds of behavior?

Like tampering with the twenty-four-hour cycle, so firmly bound to the nature of our earth and our bodies, a manipulation of rate is likely to be a most difficult change of time structure. If any locality or group has a rate of change which is consistently slower or faster than its surroundings, it will be isolated or overwhelmed. Whether we have the power to manipulate rates of change consistently throughout a society is very doubtful, nor are we yet wise enough to identify optimum rates. Decelerated areas might survive for a limited period and might be appropriate refuges for those bewildered by the normal pace of change. Certain religious communities, old residential areas, or "backward regions" have this characteristic. They are admirable if membership is voluntary (but it often is not) and if there is a mechanism for an eventual catching up.

As one possible suggestion, some areas might be systematically retarded—that is, they would change at the same general rate as the surrounding society but would consider whether to accept some changes only after a standard period of delay. Introducing the automobile twenty years late, for example, and then only in some modified way as suggested by experience, might have been a canny policy. A calmer pace would be the result of this comparative lateness, and the possibility of avoiding changes that had proved to be undesirable would be a solid advantage. Pace could also be retarded by damping the rate of transmission of information: substituting the weekly for the daily newspaper, or mail for the telephone.

The opposite possibility is a future-oriented region, always experimenting with foreseeable changes before they generally take hold, thus speeding the rate of change by trying many new articles or behaviors while constantly discarding those that do not prove viable. Similarly, the circulation of information can be stepped up. Indeed, the worlds of fashion, or of center-city high society, have some of this character.

Both these states would be artificial ones, maintained at a cost. They could not be completely consistent. A retarded area, for example, could not easily exclude a newly proved cancer preventive. Yet, within reason, if members were voluntary participants and willing to bear the cost, certain manipulations of the change rate might be welcome.

There could also be special environments for people who are present-oriented by temperament: microworlds characterized by direct decisions, frequent holidays and events, mobility, short preparations and quick payoffs, opportunities to become competent rapidly, happenings and spontaneous gatherings, reversals of time structure, brief contracts and affiliations, chance meetings and opportunities, a fluid social pattern. Less would be collected or remembered there, and the spontaneous grace of free, irregular group time could be enjoyed. There are advantages in close but temporary interpersonal relations. A chance-met stranger will tell someone the story of his life. Commitment and intimacy need not depend entirely on the duration of a relationship.

These are the characteristics of holiday resorts,

"crash pads," and "instant communities"—the locales for existential acts. But unless temporary, these features must also be accompanied by some movement toward a new, stable pattern, some encouragement to enlarge the psychological present, to connect it with past and future. Such features are prominent in the experimental life-styles of young people today. Dropping out is a flight from rigid urban time patterns; turning on is a search for an (illusory) timelessness and a deep immersion in present rhythms.

Some experiments with shifts in period or cycle could perhaps be made. For biological and climatic reasons, we are unlikely to escape the dominant diurnal and annual rhythms, but a slower or more rapid but still congruent cycling is quite possible within those rhythms. There is some evidence of a natural ninety-minute rhythm of arousal and attention, for example. The rhythm of the week is completely artificial, with a historical but now irrelevant religious and economic basis. Other cultures have used quite different schedules. The Romans counted the days backward from the ides and nones of the month, toward which time seemed to stream forward. This view implied a greater temporal extension than in our system and a clearer focus on key points. The Luvale people in Zambia use an eleven-day moving period: today plus four days backward and six days forward.

Reference 17

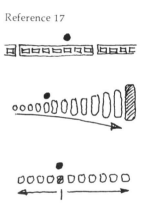

The modification of our week would be difficult simply because of the great number of activities coordinated with it, yet it would be interesting to know if a different cycle of work and rest, or even a noncyclical system, would be preferable for some people. The four-day work week is now appearing in the United States. Experiments in time organization are being made in the Synanon community (the experimental group that began with drug withdrawal), for another example. In one of these experiments, a group is divided in half. One half works intensively, fourteen hours a day, to support the other half, the members of which are free to think and dream. After a period the assignments are reversed. Learning and production may be more efficient if pursued in bursts longer or shorter than the customary ones, although rapid changes of schedule may exert stress on the body. Regularity may have a biological basis.

Although time packaging may need to be fine in some areas of behavior, it can be coarse and indistinct in others. It was not so long ago that time was reckoned only to the nearest hour. We often use a coarse grain on social occasions, while pretending to refer to finely divided clock time and feeling guilty for the deception. Indeed, different activities are organized into periods in which time has different values and is constructed differently. In team sports, for example; there is the twenty-minute hockey period, the fifteen-minute football quarter, the twelve-minute basketball period, and the baseball inning of no set length. The pace of the whole, the cycles within it, the variations in intensity of action, all are peculiar to the specific game. On the borders of all time packages there are neutral zones, small bonuses, in which time can be used luxuriously without "wasting" it. I argue here for a looser grain of time, highlighted by occasional moments of fine, sharp division.

The most common stress is synchronization, coordinating our time with another person's time, except in those joyful moments when we truly work together. Maurice O'Sullivan, writing of his boyhood off the Irish coast, tells of his first trip to Dublin and of how the scheduling of the trains terrified him. Synchronization on his own island had been simple and coarse, signaled by the changes of daylight and made possible by patient waiting.

Synchronization often weighs on us. Acting together may be a pleasant thing: in dances, in ceremonies, in music, in rhythmic physical labor. But when action is prolonged and not reinforced by direct rhythms or by the sight of others acting in concert, the imposition of outside time is oppressive. Eating, rising, resting at the same hour may suit neither our enduring nor our immediate preferences. Even our vacations are temporally ruled, and one of the pleasures of a late night party or a very early rising is in the sense of escape from time. One advantage of a life devoted to individual artistic creation, or of being a gypsy, is that it allows a "free-running" schedule. Yet social coordination depends on synchronization,

Reference 83

and without some determinate timing individual behavior is disoriented as well.

In large cities the volume of services and facilities required allows them to accommodate certain differences in timing, or even to be available on a twenty-four-hour basis, taking advantage of statistical regularities to predict the loads. For each time preference there exists a sufficiently large group with whom one can synchronize one's own behavior. A collateral advantage is that peak loadings are smoothed out and facilities more efficiently used. Urban designers often propose localized twenty-four-hour environments, active at all times. This objective may be less important than seeing that specific activities are always somewhere available. Morning and evening people can then coexist, and each can leap the fence into another time pattern if he desires.

The medieval city was the polar opposite: in Florence it was assumed that only criminals were out at night, and nocturnal pedestrians were arrested. In our own day, decreasing street safety again restricts timing freedom. People feel secure outdoors only at conventional hours, when they are convoyed by the presence of others. The twenty-four-hour restaurant and the street life of the university neighborhoods of the thirties may be fading again into medieval night.

Attempts to formalize multiple scheduling have not been very successful. A rotating five-day week was instituted in the early years of the Soviet Union to promote efficient use of physical resources, but it was soon abandoned. The aim was efficiency and not freedom: individuals were fixed into weekly cycles that were abstractly out of phase but not qualitatively different, yet they had to suffer all the disadvantages of a lack of synchronism with others. In the United States some staggering of work-leaving times occurs spontaneously, as people adjust to commuter congestion, but measures to impose staggered hours are met with resistance. Night production shifts and special night or holiday services are now common. Large shops are opening on Sunday. In some cases these changes make a welcome fit with the time preferences of the worker as well as the person served, but more often they impose a biological and social burden on the night worker and are considered less than desirable by him (though this attitude could change if the same activities and services were available to the night as to the day worker). Holidays are no longer taken in a single customary period; they are spreading throughout the year. The four-day work week may ease the weekend traffic jam. Perhaps synchronization *is* slipping its hold.

Neither synchronization nor multiple scheduling should be imposed unnecessarily since the timing of behavior is so highly personal in nature. Where synchronization is absolutely required, it should be supported by perceptual clues that convey the sense of common endeavor. When concerted effort is needed to move a weight, a rhythmic song makes it jump. When a group deliberates together, a token meal can prepare everyone to think in concert. It is an important principle that the synchronization required in production need not be carried into other realms, and indeed production itself can be modified. Absolute coordination may be eased by agreements about overlap periods in which all elements of the work force are present, the remaining hours to be allocated optionally. Western society has tended to be much more rigid temporally than is necessary. It has uncritically taken into other areas of existence the strict requirements of its production lines. Even in production we hope for a time when, as machines become more finely synchronized, men need be less so.

Basic services should be continuously available. Information as to the timing of events should be accessible and innovations in time styles encouraged or at least tolerated. The off-hour noise or loss of privacy that annoys us when schedules are out of phase must be subdued by environmental barriers or behavioral rules. For occasional use, special regions could be established where not only all services were available at all hours but where no time schedules or even time signals were imposed, so that individuals could follow any rhythm at will. Such temporal retreats could be used only periodically or when one had a powerful self-generated task to accomplish, since otherwise the breakdown of time discipline might be shattering. An opposite kind of retreat would be one in which activity timing was completely fixed; there would be no "free" or "empty" time and no choices to be made. Such areas would shelter those who sought relief from the responsibilities of timing, by enfolding them in an environment in which (like the summer camp or the monastery) all was prescribed.

But we want to celebrate time, not simply to   **Celebrating Time**
organize it. Certain locales where the activities of many workers or strangers must be coordinated will always require ample references to abstract time. (Computer programmers call this scientific abstraction "real time"!) Elsewhere, we may look for more congenial indications of the passage of time, chains of notable events and culminations, moments when we feel alive in the fullest sense, separated by background periods of imprecise duration and slower tempo.

We take pleasure in distinctive events, as in distinctive places. Important hours should be perceptually remarkable, and then we can find our way in time. Places and events can be designed to enlarge our sense of the present, either by their own vivid characters or as they heighten our perception of the contained activity—setting off the people in a parade, an audience, or a market. Places can be given a particular look at particular times. It was a nineteenth-century tradition, for example, to set out seasonally changing displays of flowers in public parks and even to lay out a garden in which different species opened and closed their blossoms at regular intervals throughout the day. Flowers, grown to be seen and to synchronize the actions of insects, are natural time markers. Old holidays retain special flavors, although the customary types of behavior that accompanied them were at one time more distinctive. But supermarket food no longer reflects the season.

Common events are not created by fiat (think of Father's Day or Library Week), but existing and emerging ones may be supported by judicious regulations or by a setting—by special lighting or decoration, by concentrations of activity, by official closing hours, even by special locales reserved for a particular occasion. Certain open areas might be accessible only on particular days, for example. In one student's memory of childhood, the most vivid feature was the "Easter House": grandfather's house and yard, visited only for the yearly Easter egg hunt. The distinctiveness of a place—large, overgrown, full of strange objects—fused uniquely with a special occasion of excitement and search, and the gathering of the clan. Or listen to an Ewe chief, speaking of the old village from which his people had been driven by the waters as they gathered behind the Volta dam in Ghana:

He looked down at his feet and seldom raised his eyes. . . . In the old village . . . the villagers would go to this [special] grove of trees only on this day of the year to commune with the spirits of their ancestors, those who are dead and those who are yet unborn. . . . The whole family, past, present and future, [was] together in this special place at this special time. . . . They belonged to the land and the land belonged to them. . . . They belonged to their ancestors and their ancestors belonged to them. They belonged to their children yet unborn and the children yet unborn were there in that land. . . . [Now] their old ways were gone. . . . The comforting things were no longer around them. . . . Grandchildren were being born in cities far away, grandchildren they had never seen. . . .

Special arrangements could support celebrations occurring in our cities today, rising out of the real mishaps and delights of our times: the weekend parades on King's Road or Sunset Boulevard, the important concerts or athletic events, the divisions in the academic calendar, the political demonstrations, the coffee breaks, the anniversaries of war and assassination, the summer holidays. The events of smaller groups could also be marked in the streets, and special games or food or costumes appropriate to them could be prepared. We should be increasing the density of special events in our lives, not decreasing them as we do. It is not merely nostalgia that makes our childhoods seem richer in this regard.

At times we enjoy complete immersion in immediate sensation. Music, dance, sports, or any action that engages the whole body can do this.

Figure 24
The memorial exhibition created over the weekend at M.I.T. to express the common sense of loss at the assassination of Martin Luther King.

Figure 25
A sense of the present can arise from a contrast of meanings.

Figure 26
A kite festival makes a
memorable present.

Reference 100

Creative work or intense perception will do the same. For the moment we are free from regret for the past and anxiety for the future. Perception and response are focused. Environments can aid this immersion not simply by removing distractions but more effectively by vividly engaging our awareness. There can be sanctuaries, surprises, strange information, or beautiful things in hidden places.

We remember with pleasure the sudden evenings that follow the long summer afternoons and will be followed by slow nights. There is a special poignancy in the moment of transition, which has its analogue in the pleasure of lingering in a doorway, the transition between spaces. The coming of the Midwestern spring, the setting of the sun, the turning of the leaves in New England, the arrival of the first heavy snow, all heighten the sense of the passage of time. As the architect clarifies and embellishes spatial transitions, so perhaps the environment should not be temporally changeless or change evenly with the clock but should seem to make dramatic transitions, succeeded by slow shifts. New rituals of time might arise: letting in the light, celebrating the solstice, dramatizing a residential move, marking birth and death. Beginnings and endings are what we remember in order to make sense of the drift of events. Some changes should coincide with social transitions: marriage, closing time, mealtime. The course of the year might become a succession of distinct periods on the background of neutral time. The standard hour and the standard week were important achievements. Can we now create a more human calendar?

In the Renaissance the design of pageants, processions, and spectacles was an important function. The English monarchy had its Office of the Revels. Expert designers were employed and large sums expended. The masques of Elizabeth's day and of the Stuart monarchy up to the coming of Cromwell were elaborate affairs, "pictures with light and motion." Clouds moved and opened, and there was layer on layer of scenery, massive machinery. The effects were most stupendous just as the monarchy was collapsing (this fact may conceal a warning). Contemporary artists (also in a time of political turmoil) are similarly interested in making the present vivid. They are fascinated with improvisation, audience participation, performer-organized music, happenings, responsive or self-destroying sculpture, computerized light environments. Architects are becoming interested in temporary structures. Protesting against the weight of the Italian past, Sant'Elia proclaims: "We now prefer what is light, ephemeral, quick. . . . Our houses will not outlive their tenants. Every generation will build its own city." Today one can buy paper wedding gowns and convert them to kitchen curtains afterward. Reference 38

Fireworks displays have the same fascination. In Valencia, the *falla*—large and elaborate topical sculptures of wood and papier-mâché—are erected on the street corners in the spring and then burned during a night of celebration. They originated with the medieval carpenters who made rough wooden scaffolds to hold candles for work in the winter darkness and burned their frames to welcome the spring light. In a similar vein, revolutionary societies such as Cuba, and the Soviet Union in the early days, devoted much energy to social celebrations of release and hope for the future.

There is an excitement in impermanence; evanescence is a moving thing. Young people want to feel themselves alive now and to celebrate their lives. They build sculptures out of waste materials on the mud flats of San Francisco Bay. Chalked on a railroad footbridge in London was the question "Is there a life before death?"

As Richard Neutra said, reactions and pleasures are time-stratified, some sudden and passing, some steady and everyday. There are both ephemeral and durable environments, and each requires different modes of design. The conscious design of special events is being practiced again in the summer festivals, the demonstrations. We are, of course, already accustomed to such ceremonial managers as caterers, undertakers, banquet directors, ministers, play leaders, but the ceremonies they manage are routinized and use standard environments and permanent props. An event designer would be charged with creating an array of occasions, designing the environment, arranging the Reference 79 details, supporting and suggesting possibilities for the actions themselves. He would be competent in the suitable media: dancing, acting, singing, cooking, cinema, sound and light environments, fireworks, graphics, scene design, games, storytelling, music, ritual, sports. He would be skilled in timing, in organization and the means of evoking participation, competent to initiate and support a shared creation of environment. He would be a temporary environmental manager, hired for the occasion and able to build and to sustain a professional reputation thereby. If there is danger of losing spontaneity by this device, there are also great possibilities for enrichment from it. In a complex society, spontaneity is not often encountered. Indeed, even those who are spontaneous largely follow ritual models of spontaneity. A planned model may elicit spontaneity rather than suppress it. (But the creation of temporary environment must also include its removal, perhaps its ritualized removal. How stale it is, the morning after!)

Periodically, we want to enjoy a common, vivid present, enlarged by group expectations and memories. While the possibility of doing so depends on common aspirations and a common history, environmental management can facilitate it. If forms are standard and do not change, we experience *déjà vu*. The world recycles endlessly. Pervasive novelty is even more disturbing. We experience *jamais vu* — we see nothing we have ever seen before, there are no connections, the present is perilously small. Without a formal organization of time and disdainful of those who are bound by it, gypsies seem to live from one spontaneous celebration to another, brought on by chance encounters at the crossroads of the world. But each celebration is also a nostalgic festival, which reaches back to memories of the dead kin mutually known to those who have met together. As we shall see, past and future time may be "borrowed" to enlarge a present, just as we "borrow" outside space to enlarge a small locality.

Temporal territories peculiar to a group can be established, just as we establish spatial territories. Form can dramatize activity as well as support it. We can be given a sense of how our time fits with the time of other people and other living things. Environment can make us aware of being alive now and together in a common present, in which we sense the flow of events and to which we can attach our hopes and fears.

We act now, modifying our environment for the future. We recall now. We learn now, which is to say we modify ourselves to act more effectively in the future. An environment that facilitates recalling and learning is a way of linking the living moment to a wide span of time. Being alive is being awake in the present, secure in our ability to continue but alert to the new things that come streaming by. We feel our own rhythm, and feel also that it is part of the rhythm of the world. It is when local time, local place, and our own selves are secure that we are ready to face challenge, complexity, vast space, and the enormous future.

4

The Future Preserved

The black industrial town of Middlesbrough was built with driving speed in the 1840s to support the new factories that sprang up along the canal. Houses and mills were provided instantly; institutions, utilities, and other amenities came later. Speaking at the fifty-year jubilee in 1881, an orator said that the founders of the town had put their trust in the future:

Reference 33

The steam engine had no precedent, the locomotive was without ancestry, the telegraph centered on no heritage. . . . [I have] a sneaking sympathy with the plaintive wail that Mr. Ruskin . . . so eloquently raises over a vanished and irrecoverable past. But the facts are against him.

Men look out on the future with very different eyes: some consider tomorrow or just the next hour; others are preoccupied with events a generation away. The future may seem something that lies ahead of us, something to be explored with hope and effort, or it may seem to be rushing toward us, beyond our control. It may be a realistic expectation tied to present and past experience, or it may be a disconnected fantasy of wish and fear. It may be something to avert or a promised land. A difficult future will add to present suffering or may be ignored by attending to immediate rewards. Intense experience in the present or fatigue can inhibit the creation of a mental image of the future. In return, preoccupation with the future can prevent us from

Reference 4

fully experiencing the present. These views in themselves help determine the course of future events.

Concepts of the future are affected by past experience. Both children and adults tend to have realistic short-range expectations and unrealistic long-range ones. The crucial differences between the age groups lie in the middle range, the future over which present actions have some influence but which is neither inevitable nor precisely predictable. As a person matures, acquiring more extensive past experiences, he extends his middle range of realistic expectation and distinguishes more sharply between prediction and wish. Where past experience has been stable and orderly, giving rise to progressive changes with predictable results, a future concept of greater range and realism is encouraged. Where the past has been chaotic or frozen, the individual will contract and disconnect his image of future time. But, in reverse, where the future seems inscrutable or dull, the past will also tend to seem inexplicable or empty. Both images proceed together; hope goes with nostalgia.

Since past and future are present concepts, built in similar ways out of present data and attitudes, their correspondence is not surprising. Though the two have equal reality in the mind and a parallel structure, they are quite unlike each other in the data they employ. The past is built of a multitude of experiences, continually brought to mind by institutions, by the material environment, by written records. The concept of the future feeds on thinner stuff. Not only is it objectively uncertain (and so is the past, of course, as any historian will ruefully admit), but also subjectively it seems less solid and rich. When people are asked to use their imagination to complete an unfinished story and that story is supposedly laid in the past, the tale tends to be given a rich and interesting conclusion. Yet, when people are asked to complete the same story as something that will happen in the future, the added endings will be sketchy and unreal. For an example closer to home, let the reader compare the illustrations that adorn this chapter with those associated with Chapter 2. Any efforts to increase the range and realism of the concept of future must work against this inequality.

Our power of creating a mental future lies in our ability to imagine the remote consequences of present acts, to create new combinations of act and consequence, to connect present feelings and motives to those consequences, and to suppress or to de-emphasize the present stimuli that would otherwise deflect our attention from those future events. A lobotomy of the brain will relieve tension and compulsive behavior but will also remove restraint and foresight. The future can still be conceived, if presented, but it is cut off from present emotion. Attention and action vacillate at the call of immediate stimuli.

If the image of the future depends on our internal ability to conceive and connect future consequences, it also depends on our general attitudes—a strong sense of self with its own past, present, and future; a belief that life is in some measure subject to personal control; a pragmatic view that the validity of a present action depends on its consequences in the future, realistically appraised. Thus the future may change—in its range, its relatedness, and its emotional tone—according to our conception of our present circumstances, our image of our past experience, and our general mental abilities and attitudes.

Both to improve the effectiveness of our actions and to strengthen the sense of self and its relation to the world around us, we want to increase the range and the realism of our image of the future, particularly to sharpen our sense of the middle-range future. The future action of any complex system is usually relatively unavoidable in any immediately succeeding time, owing to the inertia of the present dynamic state. Beyond that time the action can be influenced in planned ways, based on the predicted consequences of interventions in the present state. Beyond that again the consequences of the present state and of present and future intervention are too uncertain to make any directed steering possible.

Predictive accuracy is not really as necessary as a heightened awareness, an ability to readjust our image of the future as the present changes, a capacity to imagine and test new futures. We also like to hold a joyful view of things to come, but that depends on realistic circumstances. Luckily, circumstances to some extent depend on attitudes: a man who believes in his ability to change events is more likely to be able to exert some personal control. But where future possibilities are realistically unhappy, we can rationally withdraw our minds from them only if we are truly unable to change them. If San Francisco is soon likely to suffer an earthquake, we must consider whether there is any way to avert the quake or its consequences. But if we can do neither, then we cannot be criticized for living in the present. Such temporal flexibility is a gift to be prized.

The Limits of the Future

Astronomical evolution is a fascinating subject but no guide to our conduct. It is unreasonable to maximize the range of the future image: we cannot care for what is very remote. We can be locked into eternity as unhappily as we may be locked into the present. Therefore, we should increase the range of the imagined future, as well as of the imagined past, only as far as is consistent with our real power to remember, predict, and control, while remaining able to live wide open in the present and while maintaining the intellectual and emotional coherence of our whole image of time. "One can create something, it is true, which will last a thousand years, but no one can tell who will be living after a hundred. Let it suffice to create a spot for pleasure Reference 36 and ease," says an old commentary on the Chinese garden. On the other hand, the builders of the medieval cathedrals of Europe, secure in their vision of the future and of the overriding importance of what they were doing, sometimes budgeted their building programs 1000 years into the future. However jerkily, work proceeded as planned over periods longer than centuries. The rationality of action depends directly on the period for which plans and forecasts are made. Short-term madness may be long-term sense, and short-term sense may be long-term madness. In the abstract, one madness is not preferable to the other.

The optimum reach of the future will therefore change as outward circumstances change but also as we change ourselves by increasing our power to make intellectual and emotional connections. Progressively, we may learn how to humanize long stretches of time, just as we are gradually humanizing larger and larger spatial territories. Indeed, since we may now have the power to destroy human life on earth within a few generations, we must most urgently expand our care and attention to that range of space and time. Our new technical abilities for killing, pollution, or genetic modification force us to revise the range of our future image. But that range is not endlessly extendable. We should aim for a consistent fit between circumstances, power, and imaginative ability.

Working for a rationally conceived future reward, however efficient, is not as satisfying as work that seems pleasurable in itself in the present. To enjoy making chairs is more pleasant than to anticipate sitting in them. And under the stimulus of such present pleasure we shall make better chairs and work more steadily in making them. Learning for the joy of learning is a better motive than learning to get a degree to get a job. To be effective, the process of conserving the earth for future generations will have to become an activity that seems rewarding in itself, just as we have present joy in our children and grandchildren.

Wherever future consequences are stable, it is desirable to shift the affect from the symbolized consequences to the present process. Time and effort are required to internalize this present pleasure, and equal effort is needed to break it down, should the future consequences become undesirable. Where consequences are uncertain, internalizing is unwise. Professional city planners are notorious for the delight they take in making complex plans for distant ends. If they did not take that pleasure, it would be difficult for them to work for such problematic causes. Yet this self-motivating process may turn out to have no realistic result or may muddle realistic short-range decisions. If working in the present is to involve both immediate satisfactions and symbolic, distant ones, then those satisfactions must be logically compatible and emotionally linked. When the linkage from process to result is unbroken, we reconcile joy in the present with care for the future.

Frequently we have sought to increase the range and stability of our time image by constraining the future—by building eternal pyramids or by expounding some dogma of the coming messiah. Dogma, however unrealistic, can easily be constructed so that its truth cannot be tested. No matter how chaotic existence may be, a theory of salvation will seem to bring it to a satisfying conclusion. But theories of salvation lead to irrational actions, and as the theories ebb, the believer is left gasping.

An apocalyptic view of the future is another way of easing the psychological strain. The world was expected to end in the year 1000, and people did many strange things in preparation for it. Much later, the religious sect that built the famous Old Howard Theater in Boston sat confidently within its new walls for days, waiting for angels who never came. Only the site owner came, and he took the new theater off their hands. The same apocalyptic mood is abroad today, and it may have a similar denouement.

The building of a strong image of the controllable middle-range future, realistically connected to present actions, should not result in the suppression of fantasy. Fantasies of the future, as long as they are so recognized, are an enjoyment in themselves. Moreover, the creation of fantasy is a way of exploring future alternatives and suggesting new modes of action. Any open society will have some means for generating and communicating these dreams.

Thus the spatial environment need not be subjected to plans of awesome future extent. It is more rational to control the present, to act for near-future ends and to keep the longer future open, to explore new possibilities, to maintain the ability to respond to change. Environment can be a teaching device for supporting this attitude of mind, a set of clues for enlarging the future image. It can help to reduce the inequality of data available for the concepts of past and future.

The Spatial Environment as a Future Sign

For example, we could communicate, in a clear and public way, those future events that are, in fact, already predictable or controlled. Many environmental changes are in process but invisible, even though they have been determined upon and are not easily reversed. A new road may have been located, and detailed plans may be in preparation; a building is about to be erected; the site for a park has been chosen. If these projects were announced in the environment in which they were to occur, people would have a better sense of the immediate future, which otherwise appears unpredictable and frightening to them. Even if we elect to avert or modify those coming events, having them marked out for us gives us a chance to prepare our opposition. Symbolizing a change in situ is a most effective way to communicate it. I have already suggested that it is also possible to create a symbolic temporal model of the city.

Visible and relatively inexpensive signals of future action may be displayed, like the preplanting of trees in an open area intended for later residential development. Such "instant" or "token" changes are

Figure 27
The visible framework of
this owner-built house on
the outskirts of Athens is a
clear signal of his intentions for the future.

Figure 28
The early stages of a squatter settlement in Peru. The
temporary shelters predict
the form and nature of the
coming community.

Figure 29
A new office building at
Government Center,
Boston, displays the direction of its immediate future
growth and thus increases
the predictability of the
environment. But long-
range predictions may
only delude us.

"To you children of history, who, on some far-distant
day down the dim, dark corridors of time, may breach
this stone . . ."

useful to express or stimulate impending or desired changes of a more fundamental kind. A cleanup or the replanting of a park can be the first concrete step of broad community action. Clues to the future that are real objects or are tangibly connected to real objects are more effective than verbal signs. Staking out the streets in the ashes of London was a key to beginning its restoration.

We also wish to avoid the opposite error: the proclamation of something as a certainty that is in fact only a pious intention: "On this site will be erected . . . " says the sign in the weedy lot. "There's a Secure Future in Mining Today," according to the peeling billboard outside an abandoned colliery in South Lancashire. Suspicion and pessimism feed on promises not fulfilled, on wishes proclaimed as facts. Announcements must keep to near-future results that are backed by the decision and ability to carry them out. If not, at least they should distinguish hope from decision.

Yet hope is the engine of public action. If expectations are always modest and sure, there will be no motive to do larger things; if no promises are made, there can be no common action in anticipation of a result. Promising nothing is only safe. Planners or agents of revolution may deliberately raise hopes not easily fulfilled, calculating that the later threats of failure, coming at a time when many people have acquired vital interests in success, will galvanize extraordinary efforts to achieve the promise. It is a risky business, and the right balance requires nice judgment. Surely the right balance includes the communication of some hopes that are beyond the present stretch of power but express a truthful assessment of probability, and that will be followed by an open avowal if calculations fail.

More general processes of change can also be marked out on the environment. We could locate the probable near-future edge of suburbia, for example, or illustrate the probable future degree of pollution or of traffic load. While in the long range such predictions are difficult, they are rather easy in the short. Estimates of impending urban growth should be common property. Just as each locality should seem continuous with the recent past, so it should seem continuous with the near future. Every place should be made to be seen as developing, charged with predictions and intentions.

Complex, long-range actions can be designed so that each successive step visibly leads to the next one: as an expansion along a constant direction, for example, or a regular and easily conceptualized modular addition. In a study of reactions to redevelopment in Boston, Erik Svenson showed that changes easy to visualize and of understandable form in the process of execution were accepted with less distress than changes harder to comprehend, even where the former were in reality more sweeping or more damaging than the latter. Reference 101

Accurate announcement of intention by the powerful is a policy agreed to, at least for quotation, by conscientious public relations advisors. Its utility and its execution are relatively straightforward, even if it is ignored. It fits into a common picture of the natural division of society into the leaders and the led. Many agents of change prefer to work in secret, of course. Secrecy gives them short-range advantages: speed, cheap land, a disorganized opposition. While equity and democracy are direct arguments against these advantages, secrecy also often proves to be accompanied by middle-range disadvantages for the change agent himself. Confusion, suspicion, and apathy may ricochet against his own plans, which normally require large-scale cooperation or at least acquiescence. Some agencies act with deliberate mystery; many others simply do not realize the importance to their own success of a visible announcement of their intentions.

The more difficult premise is that communicating the future must be a dialogue among all those who have a stake in it. Users of a place should have a way to mark out their own intentions and expectations. Some of these will be counterplans; others will be very narrowly conceived. Residents might express what they hope to do in their own houses or where they think a new road should go. Transit riders might want to indicate where they think waiting benches should be. The techniques for managing such a dialogue have hardly been developed yet. It could easily fall into confusion, apathy, or a

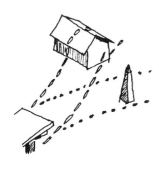

polarized battle. Conflict will be visible, and visible conflict makes us uneasy. Yet it is preferable to hidden anger.

Anything beyond the immediate future is full of uncertainty. There may be uncertainty in our predictions, doubts about what to choose, or open conflicts. Here, too, the observer can be informed by what he sees. Will it grow this way or that? Should we build this school or that one? Local residents want the road to go here, but the state wants to put it there. Every environmental possibility cannot be illustrated, or there would soon be an illegible chaos. Plural choice and uncertainty are difficult and unsettling things to express. But in addition to the sure short-range changes, we should communicate on the landscape itself some of the major middle-range alternatives and issues latent in our intentions toward the environment. How else can the citizen take part in the decisions that concern him, and learn to construct a realistic image of the future?

Communication about the common environmental future requires more than giving everyone a marking crayon or persuading change agents to be candid. Information must be actively sought out, organized, and presented. We shall have to create agencies that, like the newspaper, have an interest in communicating and a vocal clientele who will support and demand the information provided. Since only a few basic large-scale future alternatives can be clearly displayed on the setting itself, there are decisions to be made in selecting which issues are crucial and which major alternatives most likely. Selective communication is a political act, and thus any broad display of comprehensive alternatives will necessarily be controlled by the major interest groups. But this control need not prevent inhabitants from expressing their smaller-scale personal hopes and intentions—where they expect their children to live, what schools they aspire to, how the church is to be expanded. Like the marks of personal history, this is humanization of the landscape.

Forecasting

The complex techniques now used for forecasting and discounting the future open a gap between planners and the planned. A community faced by an intricate professional calculation showing that future growth will require so many lanes of new highway has no way of disputing that prediction. By its complexity, its unfamiliarity and polish, the prediction has majestic authority. It is still unclear, however, whether the new techniques of data handling will in the end serve to centralize or decentralize information. Computers may become a new weapon for elitist planners, yet they also could be used to diffuse information to everyone who needs it.

At any rate, long-range planning (and "futurism") have become anathema to those committed to democratic participation. Piecemeal change, focused on the small locality and the immediate future, is preferable when the only alternative is long-range, large-scale planning by uncontrollable central agencies. Unfortunately, many of our difficulties require large-scale, long-range action for their solution. Surely the key issue is the diffusion of control and understanding and not the temporal and spatial range of the plan. The remedy is to demystify (and sometimes debunk) sophisticated forecasting techniques and to make them available to local groups for the preparation of alternative predictions.

Forecasting and futurism are often looked upon as a way of minimizing uncertainty about the future, of foretelling what will "really happen." Some predictions are astonishingly accurate. More often, they are off the mark, but they may even be close because they were fired carelessly. I once made a population prediction that later came very close to reality but, as it appeared at that later time, did so only because it was projected from very inaccurate current data. H. G. Wells's prophecy of the urban regions of 2000 A.D. is a vision of the future Reference 107
metropolis which is uncannily true to many later features, yet it is form without substance. None of our social problems and none of the "feel" of urban life today is there. It is a typical mix of predicting and wishing and has the usual thinness of the imagined future.

In considering large social and environmental systems in which the driving forces are the wishes and concepts of large numbers of people, we may be wiser to emphasize that forecasts have another utility: they are a way of conceiving new possibilities, of acquiring new information, even of developing new values. Even false futures (despite their dangers), like fake history, may have a psychological value. Forecasting by magic, as by a reading of the *I Ching*, at least makes us feel part of the web of time and enables us to clarify hidden internal feelings about future possibilities.

Decision theory looks on the world as essentially closed, permanent, and predictable. Its model is the *game*, in which the rules are fixed and the outcomes finite. In this model, the only problems are our imperfect knowledge of possible outcomes and values and our limited ability to consider multiple alternatives. Alternatives are created outside of the game. A good decision is one that is both "correct" and achieved with a minimum consumption of time and effort.

But we actually live in a more volatile world. Individual decisions are unpredictable, since they depend on self-produced inspirations—imagined new sets of actions and outcomes. In large aggregates and for short terms, prediction may in fact be possible, since actions are in part mechanical and it takes time for creative individual decisions to affect the whole in any consistent way. But the limits are close. The visualization of the future is a creation in the present, not a transference to the present of events that already exist "out there." Seeking closure and certainty is human enough. But so is the joy of creation, of breaking out.

Conservation

Rational techniques of discounting future benefits and costs may serve for the short range, where probabilities can be assigned and alternatives are not so numerous as to prevent effective choice among them. For the long range we must look for other images of the future that will serve us better. One strategy is to find an ethical or an esthetic basis for accepting present costs to preserve future resources, even though we cannot make a numerical calculation of the present value of those future resources. We now fly in the face of Boyle Roche's famous dictum:

Reference 45

"Why should we do anything for posterity? What has posterity ever done for us?" (This is the same soaring intellect that produced the telling argument: "It would surely be better, Mr. Speaker, to give up not only a *part*, but if necessary even the *whole* of our constitution, to preserve the remainder!")

Conservation as a systematic public effort is relatively new in the West. The medieval forest laws of Europe are one exception, but even there the principal aim seems to have been to protect the royal hunt and the lord's access to forest products. mast, meat, fuel, and timber. These laws promoted conservation by exclusion: one-third of England was once in royal hands. Robin Hood, as you remember, defied those laws. But the centralized ownership that seemed to encourage care for the land was later the vehicle for swift exploitation. When kings wanted cash, the trees tumbled down.

China has an older tradition of conservation. Temple precincts and the grounds of the royal tombs were sanctuaries in which the taking of plants and animals was a crime. There were wardens of forests and waters to ensure controlled harvesting of the royal domains. Timber cropping might be regulated, fish weirs prohibited, hunting seasons established, pearl fisheries conserved, the setting of fires proscribed, or the cutting of trees forbidden to preserve the usefulness of a mountain watershed. One emperor even forbade any killing of horses, cows, mules, dogs, and chickens. These edicts, religiously motivated, were less religiously carried out. Once again, the more effective ones conserved the royal hunt, or ensured a future harvest of goods for royal consumption. North China is, in fact, now largely deforested, much of its land has eroded away, its wild species have been exterminated.

Reference 91

We are witnessing a dramatic reversal of old attitudes in Western culture: a fear that uncontrolled nature might overwhelm man and obliterate his works is giving way to its opposite. The zoos that once plundered the animal world to provide a spectacle now feel they must preserve species that are elsewhere becoming extinct.

Conservation is the maintenance in the present of resources that, it is judged, will be important even in the long-range, largely unpredictable future: avoiding the loss or degradation of goods that are rather sure to be continuously reusable, owing to certain probable limits to the variation of events. We may try to prevent soil erosion, the irreversible pollution of air or water, the defacing of some special esthetic quality in a landscape, the degradation of the human genetic pool, the extinction of other species, the loss of human knowledge or of works of art. The criteria for inclusion in this set of things to be conserved are that the resources must be ones that are likely to remain important for generations to come and that if used properly they do not waste away. In that case, a very high present cost for preserving them can be justified, even though we are unable to foresee the far future with any precision and so cannot compute the present value of the conservation.

There are other important resources that do diminish with use: minerals, energy sources. Unless we believe that they are present in overwhelming quantities (as is silicon, for example) we must moderate their present use in order to prolong their availability into the future. This may lead us to tax or otherwise raise the price of resources so as to encourage diminished consumption or the production of objects of small bulk and long life. But how far to moderate present use is a puzzle. We may simply seek to assure that those resources will be available for another generation or two, assuming this to be sufficient lead time for finding some usable substitute. Or we may attempt to localize the depletion. That suggests the creation of settlements that recycle their wastes, limit their demands, require small importations of materials and energy, and thus do not make heavy inroads on the resources of distant places—settlements, in other words, that are avaricious only of information, which does not waste in use.

Some resources are destroyed in use but can be replaced as long as no irreversible reaction occurs—trees, for example, if their cutting has not caused a loss of soil, or pure water, if pollution is not pushed beyond the sticking point. The basis for action is now again relatively clear. The first priority is to prevent the irreversible change, the second to reestablish the renewable resource for the generations of the middle future.

It is equally clear that we cannot ethically continue to store up probable disaster for the future.

What do we do with 27,000 tons of nerve gas, enough to kill the world's population a hundred times over? (This is *surplus* gas. How much more is considered "useful" and husbanded in warheads or mines?) Chemical deactivation is expensive. Packaging the gas and putting it in a pit or the deep sea is much cheaper. The containers last a reasonable time, of course, but not forever.

All these are legitimate issues of conservation. Other actions that are much more difficult to defend are carried out under the same rubric. Analyzing a capsule history of early forestry efforts, H. M. Raup observes that foresters have trouble with time because they make economic calculations on the basis of the long-future image associated with conservation. The forest is planted and tended in the secure confidence of future benefit, but the mature trees are no longer wanted. The human mind produces changes in the use of wood several times faster than the trees themselves can grow. And had the benefits of the future lumber supply been dropped from the original calculation, then quite different land management might have followed. Reference 87

Conservation easily transforms itself into conservatism, keeping things as they are: the present landscape, because we are used to looking at it, the existing customs, the current ecology. Yet these patterns are the results of continuous previous change and will change again. The hedgerows of England, now defended so valiantly against the encroachment of mechanized farming, are themselves the products of a socially damaging environmental change in the eighteenth century. The landscapes of Cuba and China are today being transformed on a vast scale, as that of the United States was in the past century. Are these changes for the worse? The delightful watery landscapes of the Norfolk Broads are the lands left derelict by medieval peat diggers. We may hesitate to change present patterns for esthetic or psychological reasons or because of the immediate social costs of the change, but we cannot raise the banner of conservation unless it is reasonable to expect an irreversible change, and particularly the permanent loss of some resource likely to be useful for long periods in the future.

Conservation has until very recently in this country been an upper-middle-class value. Often enough, it has been used to protect privileges—to keep the peasants out of the forest, the campers off the private beaches, the lower class out of the suburbs. A collision between conservation and social revolution is impending. England's industrial revolution destroyed her forests and blackened her land. As the world's population aspires to and attains the material standard of North America, the drain on the world's energy and materials and the burden of the environmental pollution that will occur in the course of this exploitation will be staggering. Yet attempts to establish international controls on pollution are interpreted by the developing countries as moves to check their necessary growth, and with some reason. Even in the United States we see that conservation measures that visibly reduce the wage earner's share or exclude him from an advance will be resisted by him. How do we make the necessary social transition without disaster? The environmental limits appropriate to affluent countries cannot be imposed elsewhere until we are willing to share our resources as well. Western industrial growth is a poor model to follow, but a turnaround requires far-reaching changes in the developed countries.

The principles of ecology are often cited as a proper guide to environmental decisions. Knowledge about the far-reaching interrelations among living organisms, and between them and their habitats, is certainly of great value in assessing the likely outcomes of action, or at least in making us sensitive to the unexpected system-wide reactions that may accompany action. But, as the source of an ethic, the science of ecology is no great help. The concept of a mature ecology—a diverse, stable system that is producing a maximum biomass or energy exchange—does not correspond to any human paradise. It may include mosquitoes, tangles of rotting vegetation, an uncomfortable microclimate, and scant production of human food. Moreover, we cannot accept stability. The world must change for us.

In the long run the proper ethical view surely sees man as part of nature and man's role as one of living together with other species in some reciprocal relationship, concerned for them, helping them and the entire ecological system to change and develop in some selective direction. But the basis for selection and mutuality is not yet clear. For the present we must rely on man-oriented conservation, that is, on saving resources of long-range value for human purposes and on a wary avoidance of irreversibility. This by no means implies a necessity of keeping the world as it is, though it is possible that care for the environment might help to smooth out the turbulence of social change, acting as a flywheel, a restraint on precipitate action. Whatever our final ethic may be, it is clear that the principles of conservation cannot solely be derived from the physical nature of the universe but must also deal with human hopes and values. And a look at the environmental situation in the developed countries should convince us that the social change we desire should not entail a worldwide diffusion of North American values and standards.

 Environmental adaptability is another way of keeping the future open. We often find that previous development becomes an obstacle to the achievement of some state later desired. While it is true that the prior organization of the setting has rarely absolutely prevented further change, nevertheless it sometimes imposes a high cost on that change or deflects it in undesirable ways. Built for a capitalist society, Havana is difficult to adapt to socialist purposes. Burned London widened its streets up from Thameside only to find that supplies then came by wagon rather than by barge, and the resulting traffic choked the unwidened lanes leading from the landward gates. Although he later recants, a protagonist in *The House of the Seven Gables* attacks the ideal of permanence:

Adaptability

We shall live to see the day, I trust, when no man shall build his house for posterity. . . . He might just as reasonably order a durable suit of clothes . . . so that his great-grandchildren should cut precisely the same figure in the world. . . . I doubt whether even one public edifice . . . should be built of such permanent materials. . . . Better that they should crumble to ruin, once in twenty years or thereabouts, as a hint to the people to reform the institutions which they symbolize.

Reference 59

Reference 75

If we can accurately foresee a coming change, preparing for that change in the present is a straightforward technical problem, no more difficult than the systematic scheduling of the development operation itself. Suppose, however, that we want to reduce future obstacles, even though we cannot specify what they might be obstacles to. This kind of generalized adaptability is, in a strict sense, impossible to achieve since it cannot be measured or tested. But in a loose way, assuming that future changes are likely to be roughly similar to past ones, we can look to see what historical conditions have allowed subsequent change to occur more easily. Often these have been the situations where there was excess capacity in the beginning: extra space, oversized pipes, massive structure or foundations. The Quabbin Reservoir in central Massachusetts was thought to be "idiotically" oversized. As a result, Boston was for decades one of the few American metropolitan regions without a water problem. New Haven grew by filling in its original low-density open blocks. Although excess capacity means additional present costs, it may often prove that the additional costs are very small for the adaptability gained, particularly in the case of low density and the excess space it provides.

Generous communications facilities, which allow people, goods, wastes, and ideas to be moved about quickly, are a second means of achieving adaptability. Unlike the excess capacity referred to earlier, ample communications facilities have no tendency to be used up with time and may have clear present advantages as well. Large cities, with their enriched communication networks, are notoriously resilient. It was London's sea and land connections that helped it to recover quickly from the Great Fire.

Third, we may spatially separate elements likely to change from those unlikely to change, as when supporting columns are widely spaced in long-span buildings and are segregated from non-bearing walls or when relatively stable residences are separated from changeable commercial premises in cities. The effectiveness of this device depends on our ability to distinguish the changeable element from the stable one. The ideal city plans that, in the name of adaptability, propose a megastructure of transportation channels within which building elements may come and go forget that transportation is one of the more rapidly shifting urban technologies. Rights-of-way are quite likely to have a long-time usefulness, but specific types of roads do not. The designers may have separated and fixed the wrong element. It is the residential unit that is likely to have a longer useful life. A variant way of distinguishing the relatively changeable from the relatively persistent element is to design as much as we can in stand-alone increments. That is, the units used in normal development decisions should as far as possible be made independent of one another. For this reason, single-family houses are easier to remodel than condominium apartments.

"Growth forms" are a fourth strategy: space for growth is left at ends or sides or within sectors. Temporary or mobile elements, additive or modular structures, or unspecialized forms can also be used. Temporary elements are appropriate only when the short life of a facility is clearly predictable and it is markedly cheaper to build an ephemeral form— where a tent will do in place of a house. More often, the acceptable temporary environment is not much less costly than its permanent counterpart. Modular and mobile structures are useful when we are sure that the module or the mobile unit itself will remain permanently useful. Unspecialized form is very difficult to define, although it may be possible to calculate the difficulty of reconverting various forms (room sizes, spans, site layouts) to a set of probable new uses or to find from history which earlier forms were most easily adaptable. Studying the history of British hospitals, for example, Peter Cowan found that rooms ranging in size from 120 to 150 square feet   Reference 43 were those most easily converted to a wide range of new uses. Smaller rooms tended to resist conversion except for a few new uses, and the number of new activities for which larger ones were reusable did not increase much despite the increase in size.

A highly adaptable environment may entail psychological as well as economic costs: uncertainty and neutrality of form can disturb behavior and the environmental image. Special measures are required to prevent this or to teach people how to be comfortable in an adaptable setting. Stable symbolic focuses—a church, a rock, an ancient tree—can help to "hold" a shifting scene. Visible continuity with the close-in, and therefore relatively certain, future can also convey a sense of security. And to some degree people can learn to take pleasure in possibility and surprise.

The provision of physical adaptability, however desirable, is a somewhat baffling subject. It may be just as effective to increase the efficiency of our techniques of physical demolition and remodeling. It is certainly as important, perhaps more important, to improve the process of control and decision by which environment is constantly being replanned. Reducing the lead time between challenge and response, establishing rapid and effective monitoring and control, contingency planning, decentralizing decision to the points of best information, experimenting, and developing testable alternatives may do more for adaptability than will the original physical characteristics of the thing to be adapted, although the latter is not a negligible quality. And when we discuss the strategy of replanning, we have come back once more to mental habits of conceiving change.

We could, for example, make explicit provision for regeneration in the construction and operation of our structures: design them to be easy to wreck or remodel, or require that a fund be established for reconditioning a site to an open and ecologically stable state as a regular part of the process of amortization. We are coming to this technique as a means of dealing with dramatic examples of degradation such as strip mining. In Great Britain a charge is levied on each ton of iron ore extracted and paid into a fund used for reclaiming the surface after the ore has been stripped away. The device could be applied much more generally. Such a fund requires that it be possible to make a reasonable estimate of future restoration costs, however.

Industrial waste heaps and abandoned city buildings spring naturally to mind when one considers failures of disposal, but exhausted farms and old military sites are more common. One of the great

Figure 30
An ancient tree confers a
sense of continuity on the
changing settlement
around it.

wastes of war and preparation for war has been its pollution of the land. War deforests it, litters it with poisons or explosives, sterilizes large tracts in artillery and bombing ranges, tank grounds, and old fortifications. The enormous area of military reservations in the United States (20 million acres, 1 percent of the nation and almost 10 percent of the land in metropolitan areas) is equal to a small nation, a Portugal, of wasted space. In Great Britain the Ministry of Defence holds over five times as much land as is officially accounted to be derelict owing to industrial or mining exploitation.

Reference 97

Reference 29

Obsolete environment, like refuse or scrap cars, is a type of pollution, a cost that should be borne by the stream of users rather than by the latest heir. There must be ways of clearing and reassembling sites after they have been used, since intensive use most typically devolves into small-scale control. One way might be the periodic nationalization of areas ripe for new development, like the suburban growth areas of North American cities. Or long leases might be used as a means of bringing ownership back into community hands from time to time or into the hands of a large agency or owner with the motive and capital for comprehensive renewal. Perhaps, at least in certain areas, land should not be owned in perpetuity but rather be granted to the individual by the community as a life estate, on payment of an annual rent or tax, land and structures returning to the community on the owner's death. Provisions would have to be made for dependents and for minimum amortization of structures. We need a self-terminating environment, just as we need self-terminating institutions.

Useful adaptability is not eternal neutral plasticity but rather the current maintenance of a continuing capability to respond to change so as to achieve changing objectives. It might best be measured as the cost of converting present elements of the environment to likely future uses in relation to the cost of providing for those future uses if one were beginning with an undeveloped site. The index, while comparable at any one point of time, will shift constantly as costs and likely future uses shift. Typical costs for increasing the index in an area or for achieving a desirable index in a new area could also be calculated, and thus a measurable criterion could be introduced into a cost-benefit analysis.

Adaptation and conservation need psychological support as well as an ethical base. Open-ended change will continue to frighten us until we have the attitudes that make it seem natural and comfortable. Aspiration and a sense of continuity are a necessity. If we are not to find those hopes and connections in some remote dead past, neither should we look for them in a remote future—some eternal goal toward which we steer but never reach. Continuance and hope can be found in the present that is becoming and in the direction in which it is going—an oriented streaming, perpetually renewed. "The road is part of the destination," is a saying of the Lowara gypsies. Death, waste, and decay are an integral part of that becoming. Dying, then, must not be papered over, nor should trash dumps be hidden sores. We need new rituals of death or of waste disposal to complement the gift giving and bright wrappers associated with new things. New and old are episodes in the flow of the stream. Moving with the stream, we look forward with anticipation and joy.

We can respond to the future not merely by **Prototypes** saving things for it and by being adaptable to it but also by creating it. While we are accustomed to making future plans, they are usually only a mix of exogenous predictions and adjustments to those predictions, or they are the organization of some new space for customary ends. We rarely explore possibilities that are genuinely new, except by accident or under special pressure or in the design of small products for sale.

Utopian visions of the future have suffered from many inadequacies, not least their thin, static uniformity. It is quickly apparent that it would be unpleasant to live there. Imaginary hells are much richer and more vivid. (Look at Dante's visions, for example. Hell and the past have all the natural advantages.) Typical utopias make no explicable connection to the present. The values they represent are circumscribed, the hopes of one small group being projected on the world. They have had little

113

effect in history, yet we continue to be drawn to the potential guiding function of these dreams of the future. Utopian ideas and experiments are alive again today. However constructed, if they are to catch our imagination, they must be more vivid and complex and fuller of the substance of the life that people know. They must rise out of today and be in motion themselves.

Would it be possible to undertake a more realistic exploration of the middle-range future? Could there be institutions that specialized in creating, testing, and communicating alternative ways of living? Prototype generators of this kind raise special problems. Whether these could in fact be devised, we do need some form of anticipatory design or invention of the future—an open laboratory for new ways of living together. Search and evaluation are the positive ways of keeping the future open, just as an image of the present as an oriented streaming is a positive attitude toward that future. They both complement the negative tools of conservation and maintenance of environmental adaptability, as well as the "objective" calculation of long-range costs and benefits. As desirable future possibilities are uncovered and their connections with the present traced out, we learn what might be done now or, at the very least, what must be done to prevent desirable opportunities from being excluded in the future. Technically, this is a more straightforward analysis than is the maintenance of generalized adaptability.

The Irrelevant Future

While attempting to keep the future open, there is no need to keep it *wide* open, able to change into anything else imaginable. Not only would that objective be prohibitively expensive and analytically impossible but the psychological strain of such an uncertain future would be more than most people could bear. Our aim will have to be more modest: first, to ensure survival (of life, of the community) under tolerable conditions and, second, to hold a few clear and desirable alternatives as open forward choices. No one can choose among infinite possibilities. Few can handle large numbers of choices, and even these do so only with great difficulty. People choose or cling to a life-style and all its interrelated ways of behaving with passionate conviction. By making one major decision, they can escape a threatening host of choices. We prefer to confine choice to a few significant alternatives, all with clearly desirable features. This will require us to give some thought to what is desirable. In what direction do we want the future to move, even if we cannot predict or control its pace or its detailed features and do not dwell on any ultimate terminus? In general terms, by desirable we mean conducive to human growth and development, open, just, engaging, and so on. But these general terms cry for extended rational and ethical consideration if they are to be connected to environment in any operational way.

Since uncertainty and the necessity of multiple choice are painful things, future certainty may sometimes be imposed arbitrarily. Contracts and laws do this, and environment can be a stabilizer as well. The new transit line anchors the community center; the new park is "forever wild." Such environmental decisions deliberately close the future instead of opening it. Closures are desirable when they conserve critical resources or eliminate damaging possibilities or reduce uncertainty and multiplicity to comprehensible dimensions or (paradoxically) preserve choices (as by saving a certain range of differentiated environment). Indeed, if and as we achieve population stability and the age distribution that goes with it, we may experience a corresponding change in the psychological climate. There may be less emphasis on innovation, and more on continuity and the stability of expectations.

But the future has many surprises, and attempts to set it in a mold may produce startling deformations: the transit line may be abandoned, illegal exploitation of the park may launch a new criminal syndicate. Our most important responsibility to the future is not to coerce it but to attend to it: to conserve our fundamental resources, create and keep open desirable forward possibilities, and maintain our ability to respond to change in the present.

These are the actions to be ethically or esthetically internalized, so that they become satisying things to do now. Collectively, they might be called "future preservation," just as an analogous activity carried out in the present is called historical preservation. And as historical preservation requires the disposal of the irrelevant past, so future preservation requires the elimination of the irrelevant future: the confusing choices, the events beyond the control of present action, the insignificant or meaningless possibilities, the arbitrary certainties, the inhuman states that are undesirable from every view. Taking pleasure in change and not simply living with it is the thing to learn—the creation and selection of branchings of the future. Young people can be trained to think of the future as possibility. They can Reference 21 analyze predictions, create novels or films of life to come, or even write their own future autobiographies. This is enrichment of the present. The world has not suddenly begun to change: it has always been changing, and perhaps no faster today than yesterday. But our attitude toward change is changing; we are learning to see, and perhaps to accept, a universe in process. We also see possibilities of some very disturbing shifts ahead: changes in society, in the family, in the human mind and body, in the inanimate and animate world around us. Everyone has a future, in the sense of events to come; what can be lost is a coherent mental view that embraces those possible events and connects them with the present. That loss is an anguish, indeed, because it is a loss of self.

Many political and social changes must occur before the image of the future can be built. Exhortation will not build it, but environment can be of some service there: present change can be made legible, past change can be explained (in place of the idyllic "once upon a time"), continuity with the near future can be displayed, conservation and adaptability can be internalized as present satisfactions, self-experiments and "museums of the future" can develop the range of choices ahead. The spatial and temporal environment can be used to shape the attitudes toward the future that are themselves keys to changing the world.

The Time Inside

5

These thoughts about how our environment represents or might represent the past, the present, and the future can be brought into better order if we look at how our bodies and our minds experience time—how time is built into us and yet also how we ourselves have created it. It is the fit of this internal time to the time outside that is the theme of this book.

Biology now reasserts the ancient emphasis on the rhythm of life. The world around us pulses in cycles great and small; we swim in a stream of time information. Some of these cycles are evident to our senses: the alternations of light and dark, of heat and cold, of sound and silence, the daily course of the sun and the phases of the moon. Of others that affect us we are unaware: the flux of gravity, of pressure, of nonvisible radiation. We change, too—we sleep or waken, are hungry or full, alert or dull, joyous or sad, are born, grow old, and die. Our internal rhythms seem to respond to the rhythms of the universe, and we use those external changes to regulate our own life processes. The internal cycles have many evidences: body temperature, excretion, brain activity, heartbeat, breathing, eye movement, menstruation, dreaming, growth, muscle tone, hormone production.

Reference 10

These rhythms have diverse periods, but in man the 24-hour, or circadian, cycle is the dominant one—the alternation of sleep and waking and all the bodily cycles attendant on those states. That cycle appears to be an inherent oscillation. Although there are individual differences in the length of the natural or "free-running" period, the variation in this period lies only between 23 and 28 hours. (The median period is close to the lunar day of 24.8 hours. Thus the earth's rotation seems to entrain us to a slightly faster cycle than our bodies might "naturally" choose!) The period can be influenced by shifts in the cycle of light and darkness or by electromagnetic fields or by social clues, but, unless externally imposed, any major departures from the normal range of that period or irregularities or sudden changes in it are always a symptom of illness. And when changes in this rhythm are imposed from outside, as in rotating work shifts or a flight across the meridians of longitude, they exact a price in fatigue, bodily upset, mental stress, or even permanent damage. In the technique of "brainwashing," for example, upsetting the awareness of the time of day is an important means of hastening breakdown and submission. There is further evidence that when external clues to the circadian beat are muted, as in winter above the polar circle, many people suffer from depression and difficulties in sleeping.

While the circadian rhythm is the dominant one, there are other important ones. The menstrual cycle is well known, but we now find that males undergo emotional and chemical cycles of roughly similar duration. There are periodic psychoses as well. Mental activity seems to peak in spring and autumn. There is some uncertain evidence of longer cycles (of disease, for example) which may be in phase with such events as the sunspot cycle of 22.3 years.

At shorter intervals, a persistent 90- to 100-minute cycle has emerged, at first in the study of sleep and dreams, and then as apparently underlying waking processes as well. It may well be a natural rhythm of the waxing and waning of attention, of bodily drive, perhaps of the processing of information. It is more rapid in infants—closer to 50 or 60 minutes. If this proves to be a fundamental waking rhythm, it may mean that the 60-minute hour, originally chosen because 60 and 24 are easily factored numbers, is an inhuman unit.

Such pulsations seem to be present in all living things and appear to have two principal functions: to keep the organism coordinated with its external environment, so that it acts at appropriate times, and to coordinate the internal flux of biological processes, so that the complicated machinery of the body works in harmony. A failure of synchronization in these rhythms disorganizes that machinery and puts the organism under severe stress.

Illness, age, and fear are usually accompanied by internal asynchronisms. Asynchronism in the external environment or a change in its phase may bring on this bodily asynchronism, as the internal rhythms adapt to the external change at different rates. Conversely, external lighting or social communications can synchronize the rhythms of groups of people, and lighting cycles can be used to reorganize irregular menstrual periods. As men free themselves from submission to the external cycles of nature, relying more often on self-created and variable social cycles, they increasingly risk internal disruption.

Rhythmic action is eagerly enjoyed by young children. It appears to be a fundamental means of orienting them to the world about them. Rhythm is connected with mental health, to learning and memory, to states of fear and security. There are individual differences in internal time structure, however, in its regularity, in its stability in the face of assault, in the length of the basic "free-running" period, in the degree to which all internal cycles are in phase, in the amplitude of the bodily changes.

Our environment subjects us to potent rhythms, many now man-created, many out of phase or experienced haphazardly. We fly from time zone to zone. Our attention ebbs in protracted meetings; after lunch we long for the nap we cannot take. We resist spring fever and fail to act energetically when we are most alert. We may be wakeful at bedtime and dull in the morning. As the seasons change, we carry out the same schedule in daylight and darkness. Our health depends on an integrated internal time structure, well joined to external periodicities. Perhaps we could begin to read the time structure proper to our own bodies. Children might be taught not only to "tell time" from the clock hands but to attend to and anticipate internal rhythms, to act in harmony with them in eating, sleeping, excretion, work, and play. As we gain conscious control of the external world, environmental time could be adjusted to fit our own human structure, while allowing more gracefully for individual variations.

Rhythms, objects, and events exist; but time and space are triumphant human inventions. Past, present, and future are created anew by each individual. At eighteen months the child will say "now," at two years "soon," and at three "tomorrow" and "yesterday." His time horizons are close, before and after are confused with spatial succession, and diverse sequences of events cannot be combined.

The Idea of Time

119

Reference 17

Time is discontinuous and linked with particular events. We are suddenly a year older on our birthday. At seven or eight years, the child takes a leap: the idea of succession is coordinated with that of duration, and different sequences can be put into a common "time."

Time is a mental device to give order to events, by identifying them as coexisting or successive. Moments do not exist in themselves; they are classes of events in which there is no need to distinguish one event as occurring before the other. We are well equipped to perceive succession and simultaneity, particularly by our sense of hearing. We are poorly equipped to perceive date and duration. Although we have internal biological clocks, they are imprecise, subject to fluctuation, or difficult to read. The structure of our brain, however, allows us to learn, recall, foretell, and create a social hypothesis of time. Using this hypothesis, we modify ourselves and our surroundings to act effectively in the present.

The sense of future arises in distinguishing between purpose, effort, and result; it is the conceptual basis for action that seeks a delayed gratification. The idea of the future seems to be formed somewhat before the idea of the past in the young child's

Reference 66

mind, and the relatively broad temporal range eventually achieved is a distinctive trait of the human species. From a simple forward projection of wishes, the concept of futurity becomes a set of expectations about events to come based on regularities in events gone by. Later, the future becomes creative; new chains of events, probable or improbable, are constructed to guide present actions. In the normal course of adolescent development, these possible futures become both more extended and more reasonably connected with present constraints. Fantasies and daydreams persist, however, just as do fables and myths of the past. They seem to be a playful way of learning how to create the future. Indeed, they continue to have a useful role, partly for release and whimsy, partly for exploring the future, as long as their dissociation from present real constraints is perceived.

The sense of past, which has the original function of informing present action by experience, grows up out of the mental retention of very recent past actions, building up then to the recollection of fragmentary sequences tied together by internal associations, as well as to more playful and continuous fables, and finally to a sense of history as casually connected and temporally coordinated.

We seem to have a brief short-term memory, in which the images of current events are stored by some active recurrent process, and a long-term memory, which involves a more permanent modification of our mind in which selected events are organized into patterns so that they can be recovered without having to recapitulate all one's personal history in the sequence in which it occurred. The elimination of information from the conscious record is essential to long-term memory, since useful memories require much compression and reorganization. We take in less than we see, and remember less than we take in. Reference 7

Past and future are imaginative creations that use selected events. We can learn to extend them. In childhood, age, intoxication, or mental illness, on the other hand, we may be unable to create them. In one recognized mental condition, the affected person is unable to "fix the present." He can use old memories already created but cannot retain events experienced more than a few seconds earlier. He loses his way in time and space, mislays things and fails to recognize them, is unable to do any sustained task that requires remembering its original purpose. An old lady remembered the village of her childhood "as if she had seen it yesterday." In fact, she *had* seen it yesterday but had forgotten that. Mark Twain describes the opposite phenomenon in the pilot Brown in *Life on the Mississippi*. Brown seemed to remember everything he had ever experienced. Every memory was inescapably linked to endless chains of other memories, and he talked for hours but could finish nothing. Other pilots avoided him. In his story *Funes the Memorious* Jorge Luis Borges makes a fantasy on the same phenomenon, pushed to the extreme.

Even the present, which seems so obviously given, is a mental construction, a conscious recital to oneself of immediate events and actions, a renewable answer to the question "What am I up to?" Often enough, sleeping or waking, we have no present at all. The psychological present is not the philosopher's dimensionless moment but a space of real duration, up to five seconds in length, but more usually less than two, in which all events seem immediately present, even though their succession or their rate of change may be perceptible. Indeed, the past and the future, although they refer to more distant events, exist only in this same immediate time, as present processes of recall or anticipation. We live only in the present and in no other time: "a present of things past, a present of things present, a present of things future," as Saint Augustine describes it.

Reference 90

The psychological present is an immediate ordering of perceived events very like the immediate (and thus only apparently "real" and given) spatial ordering of visual stimuli. It is a temporal relationship created between sensory events by grouping them together as "happening now" while also conceiving them as being successive or simultaneous, stable or changing fast or slowly. Temporal perception exhibits the same figure ground, grouping and contrasting effects as does spatial perception, and seems to be similarly limited to organizing six or seven stimuli. The present can be "shortened" or "lengthened" by the attention paid to it. With organization it can include more stimuli in longer spans. Space and time are associated constructs, although the spatial concept arises earlier and more easily than the temporal one. In early life, space and time are confounded. Later, space and time are still used interchangeably to measure and symbolize each other—a habit of mind commonly manipulated in the cinema. In mental illness, disturbances of spatial and temporal integration are often associated.

Reference 4

The mental past and future may contain significant events to which close attention must be paid in order to act effectively in the present; or events with personal meanings; or events intellectually connected to the present without such strong relevance or personal reference; or, finally, events too remote or detached to seem connected to the present at all. The temporal field is analogous to the extended spatial schemata in which the immediate perception of a local place is embedded.

But unlike spatial constructs, temporal ones are less easily verified by direct perception. Thus time structure is more subject to modification by internal state or external suggestion. The location of self in time feeds on thinner stuff than the sense of place, and that may be a reason for a conscious policy of thickening the external references to time. Estimates of duration are notoriously subjective; the past seems longer the more recent it is or the more filled it is with notable events. Time "goes more quickly" for the aged. Or when internal processes speed up as in fever or in fantasy, then external events seem to occur much more slowly. Apparent duration decreases with inattention, as we are more active or act with greater success or with stronger motivation, or as perceptible changes are better organized. It is far more difficult to make a mental representation of a measure of time than of a measure of length, or to match observed durations of lengths to those mental units.

The temporal organization of memory uses external props: spatial clues, cause-and-effect relations, the memories and recitals of others, recurrent environmental events, or specialized devices such as records and calendars. Remembering depends on a context, whether internal or external. The environment in which a thing is learned becomes part of what was learned. Special mnemonic devices associate what is to be learned with vivid perceptual images. Thus S. V. Shereshevskii, who could memorize seemingly limitless numbers of words, figures, or other material, used to attach those items to shapes and arrange the shapes along an imaginary walk down Gorky Street. When he failed, it was because the image failed: "You see, it was badly lit by the Reference 7 street lamp, and I didn't notice it."

In a tale of fantasy, Gabriel García Marquez describes a universal epidemic of insomnia in the Reference 55 isolated settlement of Macondo that brings on a strange group loss of memory. This proceeds to obscure the names and then even the uses of common objects. To survive, the people of Macondo are forced to label everything with its title and a description of what it is used for. So as not to be cut off completely in the present, they go to fortune-tellers to have their pasts given by casting cards. The physical environment stabilizes behavior—not simply by the way it constrains action but also by the way it symbolizes past actions, events, and feelings:

Reference 53

This nomadic civilization throws upon personal relations a stress greater than they have ever borne before. . . . The binding force that [trees and meadows and mountains] once exercised on character must be entrusted to Love alone. May Love be equal to the task!

Past, present, and future, then, are created together and influence one another. Their span and content are affected not only by external factors such as the stability and "success" of the past experience, the symbolic security of the perceived environment, the pressures of the present, or the reasonableness of future expectations but also by internal habits of mind, by symbolic abilities, by the sense of self, and by the strength of motivation. That the vision of the future is affected by our perceived past seems obvious to us, but that the reverse is also true is more surprising. The perception of the present is strongly affected by both past and future and in turn influences what is remembered or foreseen.

Reference 102

The present directs the past as a conductor directs his musicians. He wants these or those sounds, and not others. And thus the past seems now very long, now very brief. It resounds or is muted. Only that part reverberates in the present which is needed to illuminate or to obscure it.

Memory is the basis of self-identity, as Proust set out to demonstrate; the self is a way of organizing temporal events.

This is the internal experience of time with which we are familiar: an elastic flow within an intermittent present, moving now fast, now slowly, according to biological rhythms of which we are only half aware; a highly selective, distorted, value-laden, and changeable future and past, in which strict time order is cut across by associative interpenetrations, in which there are peaks and valleys,

124

rhythms, eras, and boundary zones. Bodily health and the crucial sense of self-identity are based on the coherence of these processes. If there are periods when we are unconscious of self and the present, there are also occasions of heightened awareness—a challenging task, delightful company, religious ecstasy, esthetic contemplation. The mystic experience does not seem to be a sense of timelessness, of stoppage, but is a very intense sensation of life and flow, an expanded and continuously perceived present. Internal time is the time celebrated in literature, which opposes itself to the logical notion of abstract time—that infinite, empty medium, flowing evenly, perhaps even reversible, in which moments are identical dimensionless points, and lengths of time are precise, stable, and exactly measurable against each other. Abstract time eliminates the very sense of being a person alive. Reference 12

Group Time

Memories, expectations, and present consciousness are not just personal possessions. These temporal organizations, and thus the sense of self, are socially supported. The most direct and simple case is the small group that has actually experienced certain events together and, by constant communication and reinforcement, creates a group past and a group future, selecting, explaining, retaining, modifying. The group may be a family, a school class, a work team, or some more ephemeral body but is ultimately limited in its span to the lives of its members. There are also larger and more enduring groups whose common pasts are symbolic rather than experienced. The ancient Chinese are reputed to have had an official tribunal whose duty it was to decide what events were worth remembering and therefore worthy to be passed down to future generations. A Mandingo *griot* serves this same function: "We are vessels of speech. . . . We are the memory of mankind. . . . We teach to the vulgar just as much as we want to teach them, for it is we who keep the keys to the twelve doors of Mali. . . ." Group memories are supported by the stable features of the environment, which becomes "a spatial emblem of time." The consciousness of the group is further reinforced by ceremonies that vivify the sense of a common present. Reference 6 Reference 81

Isak Dinesen was forced to sell her African estate, and the Kikuyu living there were driven off. They pleaded to be relocated together, and she comments:

Reference 48

It is more than their land you take away. . . . It is their past as well, their roots and their identity. If they were to go away from their land, they must have people round them who had known it. . . . Then they could still, for some years, talk of the geography and history of the farm, and what one had forgotten the other would remember. As it was, they were feeling the shame of extinction falling on them.

Next, the multiple streams of collective memories must be brought into some common framework to allow coordinated social action. There arise common ways of marking and structuring time, common histories and myths, common rituals. In older societies, time is structured in a looser way than in industrialized ones, more closely connected with biological

References 30, 70, 82

rhythms and to the climatic, economic, and cultural events peculiar to the community. Time is concrete, tied to remarkable natural and human events: generations, seasons, moons, days. It is not regularly and continuously subdivided but discontinuous, marked by named times, sunset, the dry season, market day. The significant discontinuities may be reinforced by ceremony. Duration is not conceived absolutely but, if brief, is related to an action—a smoke, a day's walk—or, if longer, is measured by counting the recurrence of some cycle—full moons, sleeps, winters. These cycles seem unrelated to one another, and it is difficult to interleave separate series of events. The month is recognized before the year, since the climatic recurrence of the year is blurred and its astronomical cycle requires precise observation. The past is remembered as a series of important events, to which peripheral occurrences are attached. Anything beyond four or five years will be referred to the span of a human life, and these lives are grouped in age sets. Beyond a single generation, time fades off into durationless genealogies or timeless myths. Calculation, subdivision, and precise cycles arise later by the magical play of arithmetic in Sumer and in Maya, where the purpose of the play is religious and perhaps unconsciously esthetic.

In more intricate and heterogeneous societies, requiring high levels of impersonal coordination, time organization evolved into the precise and abstract divisions familiar to us: standard years, weeks, days, hours, minutes, seconds, microseconds. Lewis Mumford credits the mechanical clock to the Christian monastery, whose regular devotions were required for the welfare of souls in eternity. The clock, he says, "dissociated time from human events, and helped create the belief in an independent world of mathematically measurable sequences. . . . The clock, not the steam-engine, is the key machine of the industrial age." The temporal regimentation of the monastery, in which natural processes were forced into a rigid, fragmented "rule," spread to the workplace and then to all aspects of life. Punch clocks recorded factory attendance; closing hours were imposed on places of entertainment; the railroads subordinated local times to a central standard; the calendar was partly regularized. Time controls are a means of class domination over production and social behavior. The Crystal Palace Exhibition of 1851 showed an Alarum Bedstead, which first rang the waking hour, then removed the bedclothes, and finally threw the stubborn sleeper to the floor. In *Modern Times* Chaplin struggles spasmodically to keep abreast of the smooth-flowing assembly line. Even in his flight from the police he stops to punch his time card. But in Rabelais's ideal society, the Abbey of Thélème, there are no clocks, no walls, no rules.

Reference 78

Holidays and seasons progressively lose their special character and are grouped with the standard leisure periods: the weekend or the vacation. Group activity is coordinated by clock times. Most adults carry a time display piece, much as navigators in featureless terrain carry displays of abstract spatial location. The quick outward thrust of the wrist to reveal a watch otherwise so discreetly hidden is as characteristic a public gesture as are our ways of eating, smoking, or sitting down. We are subjected to intrusive time signals: bells, buzzers, and alarms. Necessary as it may be for group coordination, this imposed time weighs on us: we seek to escape it when we can, or we feel guilty for "wasting" it.

Time begins to be thought of as a commodity and, like other goods, a commodity in short supply. Time can be added, subtracted, divided, saved, lost, filled, killed, or stolen. As individuals assume multiple roles, there are difficulties of synchronization, and time boundaries become more rigid, divisions finer. Rates (of work or of driving, for example) must neither exceed nor fall below some prescribed range. Victories and records in sports are precisely timed. Children are taught to accept a determinate schedule as a necessity (but not to tell body time, or to position their present in the near past or future). As we linger at the edge of sleep, the ticking clock intrudes and will not let us go. We wake to wonder what day it is, and what time of the morning. The time disciplines of work and school (the school so often thought of simply as a preparation for work) pervade the entire society. But, as we have seen, the packaging of time which is appropriate to a factory may be quite inappropriate for other times and places as well as out of phase with our internal time structure. Even in the factory, the precise timing characteristic of machines and once necessarily demanded of massed workers may now be required only of the former.

Reference 77

While city time seems crowded, its scarcity is not the critical problem. The more severe strains accompany time *ordering:* the synchronization of moment and rate, the mismatch of subjective with abstract time, the lack of coherence or "meaning," the conflicts between the times of diverse groups. Romantic poets used free space as an image of escape from time. Some of the new communes are based on attempts to break out of those same ways of ordering. Yet the great cycles of the day, the year, the family, of life and death have been our dependable constants. As we begin to play with them, we may find both freedom and confusion.

The time structure of a culture must be loose enough to tolerate a wide diversity of group time structures. It requires widely known events as reference points, which can be the landmarks for significant change and the symbols of social cohesion. To construct such a framework, which also has room for the precise timing needed in technical functions, is

Figure 31
Automaton time directs
the race. Everyone must
run, and run together.

no easy task. In spatial organization, a common framework is more readily achieved.

Different cultures have different concepts of the embracing temporal framework into which all men are thought to be born. Mircea Eliade described the "eternal present" of primitive societies, in which the heroic past of gods and ancestors is perpetuated by ritual reenactments of their deeds, the mythical moment returns again, and men become "real" and truly themselves by becoming imitations of the archetype. In this sacred time, people act with formality and rigor or mask themselves and turn normal behavior upside down. Irreversible time is abolished and the universe preserved by perpetual re-creation. Outside these magical moments, men drop back into profane time, which is episodic, experiential, and essentially meaningless. The primitive desire for absolute time may be likened to the corresponding desire for absolute, sacred space— distinct from heterogeneous, profane space—sacred space that is stable, perfectly oriented, at the center.

In other cultures, men may hold a more pessimistic view: time is fleeting, and the future is abrupt oblivion (loss of memory, loss of hope, loss of self). We can only live in and enjoy the immediate, evanescent present. Elsewhere, again, the sense of time flowing may be softened by concepts of cyclical recurrence, borrowed from the visible cycles of astronomy or of living organisms: events succeed one another eternally, but universal permanence is maintained as they regularly repeat themselves. Or, in a more "advanced" version, the cycles recur forever, but it is possible, by virtue, sin, or magic, to escape the cycles—to step out of time into timelessness: heaven, hell, or nirvana.

History may be seen as a long ebb from a mythical golden age—time the destroyer—or as an equally inevitable progress toward higher and more complex forms—time the creator. Change and the flow of time may be accepted but with the belief that there was a definite beginning and will be an apocalyptic end—a leap into eternity. Such an apocalyptic view of the future seems to be appearing again today. Time may be thought of as linear, unchecked, impersonal, without beginning or end.

Timelessness may be sought in drugs, mysticism, or esthetic contemplation.

Alternatively, we may focus on an extended, moving zone of time whose trailing and leading edges, moving with it, fade into darkness. Gypsies Reference 23 live in such an extended present, with memories reaching back to the last ancestor they knew alive. They are without a Messianic vision or a symbolic and remote historic past. They burn the goods of a dead man and after mourning him for a period "release him from the fetters of [their] sorrow." Dead souls weaken and die once more at the death of the last person who knew them. "Life is a flow, a dialogue, and death is an isolation, a dividing."

The Hopi do not even distinguish time and space as we do. For them, the world consists of the "manifest"—the tangible, visible reality that has happened or is just happening—and the "unmani- Reference 108 fest"—the inner essence, the hope and desire in all things, not yet actual, which enters the manifest by spiritual effort. Far away and long ago are the same; they are in the manifest. Future and inner are also the same and lie in the unmanifest. All of these concepts are attempts to make an explicable order out of temporal (and spatial) events—human efforts to live with the human idea of time. These images are crucial to identity, firmly held, and their modification is fiercely resisted.

Our loss of faith in magic, inevitable progress, eternal existence, the vast perspectives of time and space opened by science, and our inability to understand history as a coherent process, all put heavy stress on our image of time, expose the individual to alienation, and tend to enclose him in a purposeless present. When we look forward or back, we no longer feel at home. There is a sharp contrast between subjective and social time. Self and time are simple commodities whose present value fluctuates.

Within a given society, there are equally sharp **Time Orientations** distinctions between the ways in which individuals or small groups conceive of time. Variations occur in basic orientation (the emphasis on past, present, or future), as well as in the extension and coherence of these images. Time horizons may vary markedly between youth and age, between lower and middle class, between illness and health. The same individual will have different time perspectives in different kinds of behavior—playing a game and buying insurance, for example. A consistently held, contracted view of time endangers learning, concerted or sustained action, and the very sense of a stable, valued self. Present-oriented life-styles have much to teach us about the joyous acceptance and celebration of the immediate world, but they have serious long-term consequences when applied to collective action.

The number and severity of changes in our personal life—from the death of a spouse to a minor move—apparently correlate with our subsequent liability to illness. Similarly, people who must cope with the shock of a major historical transition feel the disconnection of present from past or future. Radical young Japanese intellectuals look to the future as something wonderful, awesome, and limitless in time, a utopia whose qualities cannot be described. Their task is to destroy the present, to cut off the recent past, to make way for this unknown, eternal future. Young Japanese traditionalists look back to a limitless utopian past, into which they hope to transform the future again. Both groups despise the confusion of the present and the recent past. Both long to break out of time. They share a nostalgia for the deep past of childhood. One radical futurist remembers:

There is a big stream in our village. . . . I have memories of its current dashing against the rocks, and it gives me the feeling of a true river—not like those rivers we so often see. . . . In the old days the water was very abundant. . . . But now we can no longer see such a scene . . . and the water has greatly decreased.

Uprooted persons, those who suffer shock, or those whose realistic futures are terrifying or completely unpredictable, will withdraw into a narrow present. The busy, practical man may also be completely absorbed in the immediate, like E. M. Forster's Mr. Wilcox, for whom "the past flew up out of sight like a spring-blind, leaving only the last five minutes unrolled." Others will escape into temporal fantasies, while neurotics may be so preoccupied

Reference 53

with past or future as to be unable to act effectively in the present.

Eugene Minkowski writes of the intimate relation of psychosis to disorders of the image of time and describes several categories of temporal disorder. One depressed patient tells him: "I am obsessed by the past. . . . I am never in the present. . . . I see in advance how things will go. . . . I only move in the idea of movement that will follow." Another is morbidly aware of time passing: "Drops of water make me furious because I always *have* to think 'Now a second has passed, now another one'. . . . It gets worse because the intervals I have to represent to myself become shorter and shorter." The manic consciousness, meanwhile, is the plaything of any immediate stimulus, which carries it along without purpose. It cannot create an ordered present, and it moves helplessly from one sensation or association to the next. An old lady lives in an eternal present, since she forgets events immediately, and has no concern for the future. But she is serene and adapts graciously to the momentary situations she finds herself in. The schizophrenics strive to freeze time, to reduce the world to immobile perfection. "Outside things still go on, the fruits on the trees move this way and that . . . but time does not flow for me." "I love immutable objects. . . . I will try . . . to die with the same impression with which I was born, to make circular movements." "I am like a machine that runs but does not move from its place." Even in senile dementia, the last vestiges of mental activity relate to time. In almost every broken sentence there is some expression of it.

In the 1960s, B. S. Aaronson performed some fascinating experiments in which he induced a few people, through role playing or hypnosis, to alter temporarily their images of past, present, and future. The same subjects were successively asked to erase—or to expand—one of the three categories of time and then to do the same with each possible pair of categories—twelve manipulations in all. The behavioral results were varied, striking, and profound. Obliterating the present—or both past and future together, of which at least one seems to be required to give the present meaning—caused the

Reference 14

Reference 1

p	.	f
.	.	f
p	.	.
.	p	.

133

p	P	f
p	P	F
p	p	F
p	P	F
P	p	f
P	P	f
P	p	F

most violent reaction. Subjects resisted vigorously or lapsed into catatonia. Present timelessness equaled death or madness. Expansion of the present, on the other hand, or of present and future together brought great joy and energy. When the future was made long relative to the past, involvement in the present increased. When the past was relatively long, the subjects experienced disengagement. Where both past and future were lengthened relative to the present, the subjects seemed to abandon the world of action for daydreams and obsessions. Too short a view of the future makes the present meaningless, but so may too long a view. Vast time, like vast space, is painful to bear, or at least it requires getting used to. It is a poor guide to current action.

We look for a social image of time which enlarges, celebrates, and vivifies the present, while increasing its significant connections with the past and especially with the future. We seek, with Boethius, "to hold . . . the whole fullness of life in one moment, here and now, past and present and to come." The image we seek should be consonant with what we can discover objectively about the world, not false, but also consonant with our specific human ways of thinking and feeling and organic function. It would be a guide to current action, permit coordination and diversity, but also be a basis for endowing individual and human existence with meaning. The aim of this book is modest, relative to that objective: to discuss how the form of the external environment can encourage a present-enlarging and flexible image of time, how this knowledge may be used to improve the management of environmental change, and whether the sense of environmental time may have any bearing on social or psychological change.

Boston Time

We can take firmer hold of our subject by using a specific example. In downtown Boston, signs of time are frequent along Washington Street, which even today is the main stem. Once it ran from the center far out into the countryside, connecting the peninsular city with the mainland over a narrow neck of solid land. Eight miles out, an old stone still refers to that connection. But even the stone has been remodeled.

Now the old street is blocked at one end by the new city hall and at the other, although only temporarily, by the construction of the New England Medical Center. If we walk down it and glance up its side streets, we see time signals that are displayed to thousands of people.

Figure 32

Figure 33

At the northern end the Old State House is dwarfed by the office buildings of the early twentieth century, which are themselves dwarfed by the latest generation of skyscrapers. But we are reassured to see that this landmark is duly certified.

Figure 34

To many people, this building seems to be the oldest thing in the city, although it was actually built many years after the original landing.

Looking north on Washington Street from the Old State House, we see a slice of the new city hall. It faces a plaza laid out over old Scollay Square, to whose sinful memories students and other visitors are still vicariously attached.

Figure 35

And in its own day, Scollay Square had demolished what was truly the oldest structure in Boston, the "old feather store" dating from 1680.

Figure 36

On contemporary Washington Street just south of the State House, a digital clock tells us when we are to the nearest 1/1440 of a day.

Figure 37

Public clocks are constantly referred to. Even false clocks catch the eye.

Figure 38

138

If the business district lacks some of the time signals we see in the rural countryside, it is rich with the rhythmic actions of people. So there are many indicators of time on the street. In the morning and evening the traffic swells. At lunchtime the restaurants fill up. The traffic light runs slow and the parking meter fast.

Figure 39
Figure 40

People can tell time by the sun, by watching crowds and what they are carrying, by listening to the level of noise, or by seeing that shops are closed.

Figure 41

139

A few steps away from the digital clock, a broken column commemorates what once occupied this parking lot.

Figure 42

Nearby, a sign removed has left its image on the stone.

Figure 43

Spring Lane comes in on the left, and down that narrow walkway is a plaque to mark the Boston Spring, the original water source of the town. Next door, a repair shop maintains the present time.

Figure 44

Figure 45

Figure 46

At the corner of School Street, just beyond Spring Lane, the Old Corner Book Store, a thriving concern in the 1890s, still survives today in sanitized form.

The Old South Church faces that same corner, and now there is a new bank building there.

Figure 47

The Old South survives because in its time it fought off its own renewal scheme.

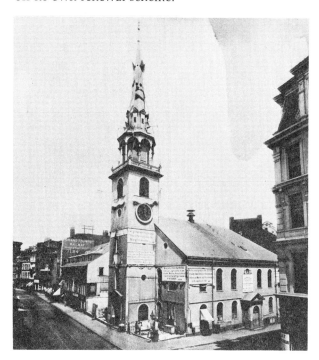

Figure 48

"Napoleon turned his great Simplon Road aside to save a tree Caesar had once mentioned. Won't you turn a street or spare a quarter of an acre to remind boys what sort of men their fathers were?"

"Never before in history has there been a nation base enough to destroy its own monuments. Never was there a country so unpatriotic as to treat slightingly memorials of the forefathers."

"Neither need greed nor the necessity of wider streets shall ever desecrate what Adams and Warren and Otis consecrated to the liberties of man."

"Think twice before you touch these walls!"

143

Preservation is strong in the Boston mind. Now no one would dare take the Common or Beacon Hill or the old churches. The next corner is Franklin Street, and two doors down a modest bust over the entrance of a blackened building marks Franklin's birthplace. But the building next door says *Transcript*, and to an older citizen this is a more poignant and personal reminder, which speaks of a vanished but well-remembered newspaper. It reminds him that this was once "Newspaper Row," where the latest bulletins were chalked on display boards along the street.

Figure 49

Moreover, historic persons are not the only ones to have their birthdays commemorated downtown.

Figure 50

A marker tells us the original name of Washington Street.

Figure 51

More recent history is set in the sidewalk, where the contractor proclaims who made the walk. It is a name familiar to those who watch the Boston ground.

Figure 52

Nearby, anonymous people have made a more personal record.

Figure 53

145

A building is coming down here, and has left the traces of its function on the surrounding walls, while a sign proclaims the future.

Figure 54

A store window also alludes to two coming events, and the brick wall next door carries an unofficial announcement.

Figure 55
Figure 56

At the central corner, time usually seems to pass rapidly.

Figure 57

But on Sunday morning there is a different sense to it.

Figure 58

Meanwhile, under the street, where people wait for trains, only clocks measure the empty passage of the hours.

Figure 59

Time also passes more slowly on the Common a block away, but here it is a calm flow, not empty or lagging. When the Common fills up for a giant demonstration, it is very different. But normally the people take their ease in season, and their clothes and their actions are a sign of the turning of the year.

Figure 60

The trees are seasonal clocks, very precise in spring
and fall.

Figure 61

In the evening, the lights come on and the city changes. For many people, this is a favorite time.

There are signs that tell the shopping hours, the subway hours, the church hours, the theater hours, the parking hours. Even the old cemetery has its appointed time.

Figure 63

Figure 64

Figure 65

Figure 66

151

A short way down the street, a hole in the shopping facade is evidence of the shift in commerce. The former subway entrances, once enclosed within a vanished structure, now set the stage for temporary market stalls.

Figure 67

Just across the street, a new subway entrance has not yet opened. The shrouded subway sign is a symbol of anticipation.

Figure 68

Perhaps the business district is slowly becoming
more remote from its users and their memories. Shopping crowds, specialty stores, and bargain basements are part of the experience of most of those who
walk down Washington Street, and part of their parents' lives as well. But the small stores and the
buildings of moderate size are giving way.

The new offices, which now comprise the bulk of the
district, are more distant emotionally. Few feel any
personal connection with these new facades. The
little open markets, in contrast, are reminders of the
past. So there is not much at the center that speaks
of a personal future. The new office towers, garages,
banks, and travel agencies are visible enough. But
most people think forward to a suburban house, or the
countryside, or another city.

Figure 69

Just beyond the market stalls, the street enters the "combat zone," that region of unsanctioned activity perched here momentarily on its long flight from the back side of Beacon Hill. Up among the billboards, however, there is still a Liberty Tree.

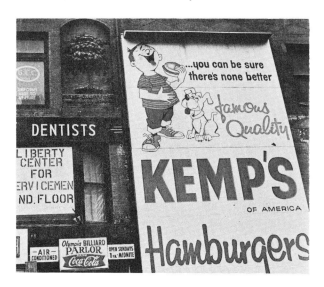

Figure 70

The lounge proclaims its late hours, and even the blowsy theater asks your age.

Figure 71
Figure 72

A sign reveals successive changes in our currency, and others chronicle political events.

Figure 73

Figure 74

The street name refers to the edge of the ancient peninsula. (If you look closely at the ground, you can trace the outline of the former shore.)

Figure 75

The sign also tells you that you are on the edge of the Chinese district, which has had its own special events.

Figure 76

(At the opposite and northern end of the street, the Italians celebrate quite different occasions.)

Figure 77

156

At the southern end, Washington Street is now blocked by the rising structures of the new medical center.

Figure 78

This is the growing end of the street. The central functions slowly pursue their course south from Scollay Square toward the Back Bay, steamrolling older buildings and activities on their way.

Figure 79

Nearby, the old waterfront is going at last, the buildings melting away.

Figure 80

The railroad, which in its day was cut ruthlessly through the close-packed docks and sailing ships, is now buried in its turn.

Figure 81

Indeed, central Boston has a peculiar air of rapid change, of confusion and excitement, unequaled since the nineteenth century, when the city was also actively rebuilding over its limited ground.

Figure 82

Figure 83

Today towers rise over the Back Bay and cast long shadows, like great sundials, or reflect older structures in their bright new mirror glass.

Figure 84

New hospital space is grafted directly on the old. A   Figure 85
burned church has not been razed, but links its new
auditorium to the surviving fabric.

Figure 86

Figure 87
Figure 88

Everywhere there are signs of time.

Change Made Visible

7

We build our image of the world with data from our senses. By presenting these data in novel patterns, artistic inventions alter our sensibilities—change what we see and therefore how we conceive the world and again how we look at it. We argue a particular aspect of this general case: that there are novel temporal manipulations of environment that will not only delight us but also vivify our image of time— help us to heal the breach between the abstract intellectual concept and our emotional sense of it.

The possibilities for temporal expression in the landscape are largely unexploited and their principles unknown. For clues, we naturally turn to other arts that have long been concerned with time.

Literature, for example, can organize the longest span that any art admits, since it may represent enormous reaches of time and may be read or heard within a lapse of days or weeks. Imaginative literature is a rich source of information about the human image of time, as this is one of its most persistent themes. But literary techniques are not relevant for us, except in the most general way. Landscape is not frozen poetry (or frozen music either), although landscape may evoke poetry or be expressed by it. Other temporal arts—dance, music, theater—occupy several hours at the most. Their temporal continuity is most like the environmental experience, and yet their techniques, if we apply them literally, are instructive only for the most rapid changes, on which an audience's attention is deliberately focused.

Painters and sculptors have at times been interested in expressing dynamic images. Turner is one example. Another is the futurists, who tried to portray the inner life of things, both animate and inanimate, and to show how it connected to its surroundings. They used distortions, interpenetrations, lines of force, violent contrasts. They broke open the contours of things and showed them in continuous motion, superimposing positions taken at different moments on the same image, just as cubists superimposed different perspectives and so represented the movement of the observer. They used a sequence of views or different figures to carry out significant

Reference 38

163

Figure 89
Giacomo Balla's *La Gior-
nata dell' Operaio* (1904)
was an early attempt by
one of the Italian futurist
painters to convey the
temporal rhythm of the
working day.

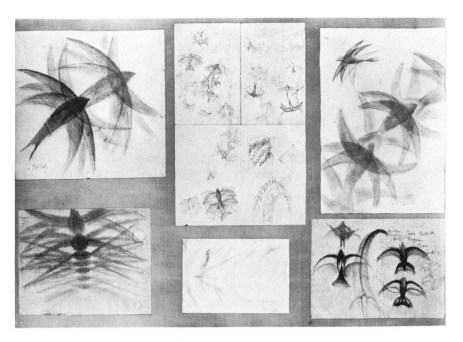

Figure 90
Later, Balla made numerous efforts to capture the dynamic changes of things, as in these studies for *Volo di Rondoni* (1913).

Figure 91
Etienne Jules Marey constructed this model of a flying gull in 1890 by reproducing in bronze the successive positions of its body and wings in space. His data came from a series of rapid-exposure photographs taken simultaneously from above, below, and the side. He thus obtained an accurate and vivid (but not continuous) four-dimensional time-space model of a dynamic action.

actions that in actuality would have occurred at different times. These devices seem so natural to us that an authentic instantaneous photograph that freezes real movement looks strangely unreal. At times we cannot sense real movements as sharply as we sense the implied motion in a single artistically selected and "falsified" moment of action.

Time is represented even in what seem to be relatively static works of art. Etienne Souriau shows that Poussin's calm *Shepherds in Arcadia* conveys the rhythm of life and death, the return to the past and the movement to the future.

Reference 96

The symphony, the film, the ballet are spread out . . . on a bed of time . . . but [plastic artists] are masters, by a more subtle magic, of an immaterial time . . . a universe whose temporal dimension can extend or contract in a moving and curious way. Now a brief and fragile moment is brought to life brilliantly, perfectly; again the extent of the universe can reach to the equivalent of eternity.

Souriau holds Kant responsible for a false contrast between the "arts of space" and the "arts of time," a distinction Kant made to give music and poetry the highest rank because of their supposed monopoly of the uniquely human realm of time. By contrast, many artists today are concerned with celebrating the present moment and its vital flow. Thus the plastic arts are rich in temporal themes, but only in special circumstances do their particular techniques apply to environmental design.

Of all the arts, film is perhaps the most instructive for us since its material basis is visible change. Its very popularity as a spectacle but also as a creative medium among serious young film makers indicates its closeness to our emerging world view. It accommodates movement in both time and space, in relation to an observer who is himself moving and changing. In film, time can be accelerated or decelerated, reversed or dwelt upon, vaulted in either direction. Each of these distortions evokes powerful emotions in the observer. Unlike literature, there are no explicit tenses or temporal conjunctions. This lack may breed confusion but confers great freedom and immediacy. As in environmental design, the potential dimensions of film are rich and complicated:

Reference 98

color, light, form, movement, narrative, sound, dialogue. Films usually tell a story, but the underlying structure is a rhythm of attention enforced by the sequence of scenes or takes. This rhythm must be appropriate to the perceptual expectations of the audience.

The juxtaposition of scenes produces associative images in the mind of the viewer. Several different times may be compressed into one brief span. Different emotional sensations are attached to spatial positions—up, down, back, front, to, from, spacious, cramped—but even more to temporal conditions—past, future, fast, slow, suspense, shock. Space and time modify each other: the idea of a space is built up by a temporal sequence of scenes; time is enriched by cramming it with spatial experience. The camera moves in both dimensions, transforming one into the other and reducing the two to emotional coherence. In all these devices, we can find useful analogies to environmental design. But there are crucial differences: in environment, attention is usually not so prolonged or predetermined, nor can the content of views usually be controlled, nor can form be so readily or rapidly manipulated.

Time has played some role in the environmental design of the past but usually a secondary or accidental one. The great exceptions are the processional settings: the approaches to gods, kings, or the dead. Most other examples of time effects in architecture are the product of chance. Landscape architecture, on the other hand, particularly in the stroll gardens of Japan and in the English romantic gardens, has developed a method of exhibiting a large landscape as a series of contrasting pictures, seen in sequence. And since those gardens deal with a living material, they have also displayed a sequence of conditions as they grew or decayed in time. These sequences have not in themselves been designed: the gardens are planned to arrive at some desired state at some particular future date, even several generations away. But old gardens often have a peculiar charm that comes with ripe maturity, and then with neglect and decay.

These examples are antecedents. If we now come to the design of environment as something organized in time or emblematic of time, we find a number of general methods available to us. One is the visible accretion of the signs of past events, which makes apparent the depth of historical time. Another is the display of recurrent, opposed states, which makes us aware of rhythmic time by contrasting the present state with remembered and expected states. Still another is the direct display of environmental change, when by transforming the scene—or shifting the viewpoint of the observer —the change can be made sufficiently palpable to be perceived in the experiential present. Finally, there may be ways of symbolically speeding or slowing otherwise imperceptible changes—changes too glacial or too feverish to be seen—so as to bring them within our perceptual grasp. All these modes have their own characters. None of them is practiced today in any systematic way. This chapter explores their potentialities.

Temporal Collage   We are familiar with the visible accumulation of historical events. The juxtaposition of old and new speaks of the passage of time, and occasionally the contrast is eloquent. The ancient Greek temples at Selinunte stand in a drift of wild flowers just opened. The Roman amphitheater in Lucca has become a ring of houses around an oval marketplace. The village of Avebury stands in a Neolithic earthwork; its houses and sheep share the space with old sarsen stones. The great cathedrals, in particular, are repositories of time. Canterbury is not so much beautiful as it is awesome—a sacred place used and added to century after century. On the north side the great edifice merges into ruins. In Syracuse the Doric bones of the cathedral protrude through its medieval skin. These are infrequent effects, not intentional, although they may be intentionally preserved once they are in existence.

Sophisticated restoration carefully differentiates modern work from genuine remains and seeks to reestablish the "real" ambience and furnishing of a structure, once having settled what the "real" time was. (Symbolic things are meant to be forever the same, while working tools are readily discarded.) Necessary new structures are required to "fit" the old, whether by outright imitation or by keeping

Figure 92
The British village of Avebury, a medieval founda-
tion, carries on its activity
within the circular earthwork and awesome sarsen
stones of prehistory. In the
middle distance is Silbury
Hill, another Neolithic
work.

some common dimension of scale or material or form. Yet secretly we enjoy the mix of old and new.

Ancient things seem most impressive in one of two contexts: either quite isolated, in some wild and lonely place, hidden or high, or in intimate contact with contemporary life, embedded at the center. There are many engaging structures in which an older framework was remodeled for contemporary use and esthetic advantage was taken of the resulting contrast of form. The new whole is more evocative than either the original building or its replacement. The partial destruction of the old center of Buda in Hungary in World War II revealed its medieval bones. Luckily, there was no attempt to rebuild it either as a medieval town or as a baroque city. Fragments of all periods were preserved. New buildings and additions in modern style that incorporated those older fragments were permitted. Nineteenth-century structures were partially rebuilt and partially remodeled. "Peepholes" on the building surfaces revealed ancient work in deeper layers.

We can imagine alterations that go further, that select and contrast historical meaning as well as visible form. The history of a place would then be not the polite introduction to a report but a series of events to be visibly illustrated and contrapuntally opposed in the construction of the new. For example, there was a proposal for the reuse of the Fortezza da Basso in Florence as a public recreation ground. Despite interesting visual contrasts between the form of the new gardens and the old defensive polygon, the dramatic historical change from fortress to pleasure ground was not made palpable in the plans. The Fortezza was an alien intrusion in the city, inserted by the Medici to keep the citizens in subjection. It is silent, ominous, closed. Opening it to public pleasure would be a complete reversal of its historic role. That reversal might be strikingly displayed, perhaps by the breaching of the wall.

This approach is not preservation, although it implies attention to history. It may mean destruction, and certainly modification. It requires an interpretation of history that may be in error and may change from generation to generation. The selection of the remains whose visual presence should be amplified is a consequence of that interpretation. "Layering" is used as a deliberate device of esthetic expression —the visible accumulation of overlapping traces from successive periods, each trace modifying and being modified by the new additions, to produce something like a collage of time. It is the sense of depth in an old city that is so intriguing. The remains uncovered imply the layers still hidden: the Roman bath and its flowing waters persist below eighteenth-century Bath; the garden mount at Canterbury, alongside the medieval wall, is a reshaping of a prehistoric tumulus.

When this idea is applied, certain past transformations are retained, others destroyed. Older features are dug out to be seen. New features are located where they produce the greatest formal and associative resonance. The total organization will be complex and informal, surprising and sometimes ambiguous. The technique implies that there must be room for new layers to come and even suggests that signs of the future, as currently interpreted, should be part of the collage. Materials should be chosen for the ways in which they stain and weather: the familiar soft gray of shingles and copper green but also the wear of steps and the way in which sootfall on deep carvings makes them appear to be lighted from below. "The more I think   Reference 93
about steel," says Robert Smithson, ". . . the more *rust* becomes the fundamental property. . . . In the technological mind rust evokes a fear of disuse, inactivity, entropy, and ruin. That steel is valued over rust is a technological value, not an artistic one." Contrasts in aging should be artistically exploited: the permanent dark hardness of flint, for example, versus the soft erosion of warm-colored brick. Near-future hopes and fears should be traced on present surfaces. Venice should be seen to be sinking. A sketch of the full-grown tree might accompany the seedling. The signs of past and future would be material for esthetic contrast and coherence. Expecting the cyclical return, Yeats rebuilt the tower at Ballylee, and then he wrote on it:

. . . and may these characters remain,   Reference 113
when all is ruin once again.

171

Figure 93
The stones of a field
boundary, locally quar-
ried, display the giant
ammonites that are part of
the geological history of
the site.

Figure 94
The vast half-buried
remains of a temple convey
another ample interval of
time: Piranesi's etching of
the sunken temple of Ves-
pasian, Rome, in 1756.

Time is "borrowed" to enlarge a present, just as it is possible visually to "borrow" a large exterior space to enlarge a small room. We propose intensifying and diversifying the sense of local time, just as we might propose intensifying and diversifying activity there. Such temporal juxtapositions can be powerful enough to evoke the sensation that past, present, and future are momentarily and mysteriously coexistent.

A technique of this kind has its dangers. It may run to a senseless contrast of picturesque fragments or even to their intentional manufacture: pseudohistorical street names or bubbly glass made on the assembly line (although it must be conceded that, for the casual and passing tourist, such manufactured history may temporarily add to his pleasure, and he may willingly submit to it). The art of temporal collage will not be eternal, since the history of today is false or irrelevant tomorrow, but then this change is also expressive of time. It is sophisticated design and demands an understanding audience. It is useful for key buildings and settings, rather than for broad application, since in most places the simple preservation of past and future traces will ensure some symbolic depth and visual resonance.

A collage is no simple mix of old and new. It is the product of esthetic judgment, the deliberate juxtaposition of seemingly disparate elements so that the form and meaning of each is amplified and yet a coherent whole is maintained. In a broader way, collage might also be used in the design of large environments: preserving and contrasting sections of different age, connecting them with paths of movement or activity links, inserting imageable new activities into older settings of contrasting meaning. The great landscape garden at Stowe, shaped over a hundred years by a succession of designers and patrons through periods of shifting taste, grew in such a way—each new design using and responding to the meaning of the previous ones. Reference 64

If temporal collage refers to progression and historic change, rhythmic recurrence conveys an even stronger intuition of time. We are accustomed to the temporal effect of episodic changes. If they are cyclical and sufficiently recent, an image of how it was and how it will be enhances the image of today.

Episodic Contrast

There is an underlying continuity of form, which takes on some new aspect in sunlight, or in winter, or when empty. These episodes are characteristic aspects, separated by rapid transitions, of an apparently timeless base form. Discontinuous recurrence is change of a kind that we prefer to see, and we often seek to cram this shifting world into that model. By sharpening a recurrence visually, we are exploiting a primitive way of sensing time. The process of change is not part of the artistic effect; it is the unique qualities of the contrasting episodes that we savor. They do not refer to change beyond our personal memories but relate to our well-remembered experience. The future is here with us because it will be like something we knew in the past.

Deciduous trees are classic examples of this effect. Their summer and winter forms are different yet logically and visually connected. Each form stands for a whole cluster of emotional meanings. Between them there are relatively rapid and striking transitions: spring buds or autumn leaves. The cycle is familiar, and in each form its shadow partner can be remembered. That rhythm has analogies to many features of human life.

We remark and enjoy many contrasts of this kind: lakes frozen or summery, Wall Street congested or deserted, an ocean shore in storm or calm, Broadway day and night. We are also impressed by changes of longer span, which are arranged in the mind as if they were sharply contrasting states: a house newly painted or shabby, a house full of children or silent. The remembered contrast resounds in the present.

We enjoy these effects as we find them; at times we create them by journalism or photography where they are barely apparent; rarely do we set out to make them in reality. But a designer might consciously seek to produce such effects. He would then consider the regular fluctuations of use or of climate that his setting is likely to endure and so order it that it will take on a distinctive and memorable aspect in each case without losing an underlying regularity. Garden architects think of their plantings at various times of year and, less frequently, under different lights. Buildings can be designed for

Figure 95
Dramatic alterations in the
sense of a place as its activity changes: the Piazza del
Campo in Siena, Italy, as it
appears when empty and
on the occasion of the wild
Palio, or annual horse race.

artificial illumination as well as for sunshine, for being empty or full, for being worn or freshly renewed. Other such feats are more difficult, for example, to create an auditorium that is distinctive and satisfying whether crowded or lightly occupied, or a parking lot or a campsite that is handsome whether occupied or not. Large environments have hardly ever been consciously considered in this way, although we enjoy some fine accidental effects. The cycles of active and quiet, night and day, hot and cold, holiday and workday, might well be celebrated at that scale.

An environment may not accept cyclical change but dramatize that change: night lighting may be arranged to reverse the shadows of the sun, acoustic surfaces shaped to amplify the sounds of after-hours passersby, activities shelters and furnishings changed to emphasize shifts in the season. Perhaps building surfaces can be invented that will respond to climatic cycles by changes in color or texture. Why not, if a landscape architect uses a tree for its brilliant autumn coloring?

People redecorate their homes periodically, and if valid techniques of interior design were more widely taught, they might be able to do so in an impressive, cyclical way. Most episodic contrasts are an acceptance and heightening of some external change. It is also possible that environments could be made to take on alternating forms without any corresponding external alteration. They would then be like natural landscapes, with rhythms of their own.

Episodic changes make an excellent background for the kind of celebrations proposed in Chapter 3. A familiar setting may be transformed to set off some special, recurrent event. The separateness of the event and yet its connection with daily life are made visible to all. School dances have done this to gymnasiums for generations, of course, and occasionally we have outdoor street dances or illuminations. Many of us carry memories of splendid festivals in foreign cities. But in the United States we are rarely willing to transform the public environment in any really striking temporary way. The tinsel hung along the light poles of shopping streets at Christmas is pitiful indeed. The fun and glitter of temporary architecture is a pleasure forgone. We only pretend to it by building elephantine world fairs that last too long.

At some time in our lives we all have experienced that peculiar sensation of a suspended moment of time, a "great present" that focuses all our attention and seems to hang motionless before us. It is an intense and mystical personal experience. Things are presented to us directly, not through the veil of customary meanings. The inside and outside worlds connect, and we seem to be the landscape itself. It is not a stoppage of time but a sense of vital stillness, wherein change and time seem immediately apprehensible. Permanence and evanescence, rapid biological rhythms and long cycles, all seem to be there together. We have constructed an unusually extended, coherent, and intense moment of present time. The experience is not readily evoked, but a powerful form or a vivid display of living things seen at some special moment can bring it on. It may happen in some cave or mountaintop or garden or by water in some very special place whose access was difficult and whose presence surprises us. Things appear fresh and new, quite strange. Gaston Bache- Reference 28 lard notes that such special places can induce this apparent stilling of time. A strong episodic setting, for example, may make it possible for us to enjoy that sense together, so that we experience again, as it were, the eternal present of primitive society.

When he has the opportunity, a skillful designer devotes particular attention to the transition between episodes. Transitions—which we call beginnings and endings—are the points by which we customarily organize the never-ceasing flow of events. Except within a limited range of rate, we are unable even to perceive a flow unless it is so marked. If it can be made sufficiently rapid and remarkable, the transition is the most evocative point of all, evanescent, ambiguous, and moving. Sunset and dawn, new leaves on bare branches, the brief fall colorings of New England, the last day of summer vacation, the gathering of the audience in the foyer or the lifting of the curtain, the homeward-bound employees released on the city streets—these are all clichés, and like good clichés they never fail to interest us.

Sometimes the designers can provide a special transitional form or may even attempt to shape the act of transformation. Redecorating itself may be made a ritual, for example.

The wrecking of a building is already a spectacle, although not one supported by any dramatic intent. The collapsing roof of a burning building, the toppling of a dynamited chimney stack are thrilling moments, even if we feel a little shame for admitting the fact. Since, as I have argued, the destruction and death of environment may be as significant a point in its process as its creation, why not celebrate that moment in some more significant way? Even further, could we design our buildings to wreck well—that is, not only to be easy to destroy but spectacular as well? (What a peculiar idea!) There could be a visible event and a suitable transformation when a place "came of age" or was about to disappear. We concentrate on inauguration so singlemindedly. But there was a famous party in the Florentine ghetto just before it was cleared away.

Some observers savor the transitions in longer processes, taking pleasure in the moment when maturity turns to decay and the fleeting nature of things is most clearly revealed. I can hardly advocate a general esthetic of decay or propose the building of sham ruins, as has been done in the past. But we might learn to see and exploit the esthetic opportunities in areas that are in decay or disrepair for reasons beyond our control. We can also make raw newness remarkable and find delight in temporary scenes. We can even imagine large environments, trailer camps or gardens, that are periodically rearranged for the esthetic impact, as well as for functional reasons.

The remembered contrast between episodes is enhanced by symbolically recalling the previous state. Japanese connoisseurs display pictures of spring in the dark of the year and snow scenes in the spring. A bare tree in a green garden recalls the winter, and a tropical greenhouse in the snow brings summer to mind. Late-hour activity is vivid when it occurs in a zone that we expect to be deserted at that hour (to come upon Yorkville in Toronto, for example). Or more abstract symbolism can be used: films,

Figure 96
Before the Florentines
razed the old ghetto of
their city in 1886, they
held a farewell party in its
empty shell by converting
it into an "Arab quarter"
for the occasion.

recordings, or other representations of former and coming conditions.

The Direct Display of Change

These are esthetic uses of a powerful and commonly acknowledged memory image of time. Environmental change may also be displayed directly, in a manner closer to the way in which it really occurs, by using the process of change itself as the artistic material. We now perceive continuous motions, rather than abruptly changing episodes, and these motions must be neither too fast nor too slow for our limited perceptual grasp. We must see or hear or feel something changing. An audience attentive to the whole process is implied, or one attentive to a good part of it. Control of all the changing dimensions is also required.

We rarely see such displays since most elements of the spatial environment cannot be changed so quickly, nor are we able to exercise delicate control over the shape of their change. The *son et lumière* shows are perhaps our most familiar example: at night, before a holiday audience, a play of artificial light and recorded sound dramatizes some historic setting. But there are simple and fascinating natural displays of change: flames, clouds, sunsets, flowing water, surf, grass rippling and reflecting the sun. The destruction of a building in a catastrophic fire or a volcanic eruption is a compelling spectacle. Fireworks, the transformation of water in fountains, or carefully staged pageants are man-made examples. Straightforward as their artistic formulas may be, these sights can be very engaging, even moving: the moment of Easter midnight in the Orthodox rite, when the new fire from the altar is passed from candle to candle through the congregation and the fluttering golden light flows out to the edges of the dark church.

These are the artistic opportunities analogous to those exploited in the cinema. Control is less strict, the audience less attentive, the effects are coarser, but for these deficiencies the scale and meaning of the elements are some compensation. Against the stable background of the permanent setting, the elements in play will be the relatively fluid ones of light, sound, smoke, water, human action, big machines. The displays must be reserved for special

180

occasions and substantial audiences. They should last no more than a few hours at most. They can use the familiar esthetic devices of temporal organization: development, retardation, climax, counterpoint, contrast, rate variation, rhythm, transition. But their structure is likely to be simple, using clear repetitive rhythms, major episodes, or growth to some climax. As objects move against each other and are sequentially lit, we may even echo some of the more startling effects of the cinema: illusions of floating or of the suspension or reversal of time. But in the public realm such willful disorientations must be gingerly done. Displays could be particularly useful where sensuous stimulation would otherwise be low or monotonous—in interior or underground environments, for example. Elsewhere, special areas may be set aside for the displays, like the pleasure gardens of eighteenth-century London, with their illuminations, concerts, plays, and dancing. An event designer might use an environmental display as a key element in his program. Pageants of the future might also be displayed.

Our technical abilities in the production of light and sound are powerful instruments for making such environmental displays. Thus far, they have been used in kinetic art and interior multimedia shows. Now we may extend them to the scale of the city. Indeed, city lights as we see them now are much more interesting than any ordinary "psychedelic" show, and the lighting of bonfires over a large terrain is an ancient act of celebration. City lights are on a grand scale, and they connect us to things of compelling interest. London's Trafalgar Square on a Saturday night is that kind of a natural spectacle. There are warm and cool lights, luminous washes, silhouettes, moving beams, colored letters, sparkling points, spotlit domes and towers. The moon hangs above, the fountains pour out liquid light, the enameled shells of cars reflect it.

City illumination could deliberately pick out the movement of traffic and trains and aircraft, flow up from landmarks, show direction, time, and weather, mark out rivers and outer limits, indicate large gatherings and important events, silhouette trees, be carried by people, contrast with moon and clouds. The many lights that go on and off or change color, dim, and brighten might all pulse according to some underlying rhythm. And the new capabilities of electronic music seem to be a peculiarly apt accompaniment to such fluid spatial appearances. Could any city sounds be so controlled? Less likely and less appealing, perhaps, but worth consideration.

The lack of detailed control may be turned to advantage, as in participative art. Major lines of development are sketched out; themes, materials, and stimuli are provided; and the work unfolds as an interaction of this original preparation with the improvised reactions of performers and audience. We can imagine an outdoor light play that is an improvisation on chance events among the lights of the city itself or on reactions of the spectators. Control may be passed to performers trained to improvise and alert to momentary chances, or to adjunct computers, or to signals from the audience.

For a smaller audience a more intimate linkage is possible. Imagine an environment that responds to the direction and steadiness of a viewer's gaze or to his vocal signals—one that is dull when unseen or unwanted but lights up to attention, affection, curiosity, or anxiety! Or imagine a small setting whose brightness, color, sound, and climate are controlled by the fine movements or even the physiological state of a single observer. This is no longer a display, something to be watched passively. The connection between man and setting would be as immediate as between musician and instrument. But complex and expensive devices, as well as trained skill, would be required. Much simpler displays would be more suitable for mass audiences.

The displays need not be purely artificial. They can be linked to natural transformations. Garden designers know how to amplify the sight and sound of flowing water. Pliant vegetation or banners make the wind visible. Flames can be lit, or the turbulent clouds brought to view with mirrors or apertures. Tidal changes can be amplified into a visible watery motion of the sea. (Oldenburg has designed a gigantic toilet float to rise and fall with the polluted Thames.) The naturally impressive

Figure 97
Claes Oldenburg altered a
tourist postcard to show
how two monumental
toilet floats might display
the rise and fall of the tidal
Thames and refer to its
pollution.

183

Reference 115

moment of sunset can be heightened by sound or by surfaces to catch and intensify the shifting color. Bells might be rung at the moment of high or low tide, or at the rising or setting of the sun or the moon. Even at less dramatic times, the changing light of the sun can be transformed by lenses, mirrors, and prisms into an iridescent display that will mark such imperceptible moments as noon, the solstice, or the equinox. And if the spectator not only watches the solar spectacle but can modify it by disturbing the apparatus, he then seems to connect himself with the motion of the planets. The rippling of reflected light from disturbed water is a familiar example of this type of partially controllable sensuous amplification.

Displays may be linked to human events as well. Light could dramatize the ebb and flow of commuter tides or make a play on the pattern of people moving in a space or on the density and destination of communications going through a switchboard. Current history might be replayed or dramatized. There could be magnified actors, flames, huge puppets. The street theaters are showing us how event and time can be brought to life in the open air by the simplest means.

Indeed, the danger lies in being seduced by the technical possibilities, thus producing striking but shapeless or extravagant spectacles. Change in the form of the large environment is bound to be clumsier and less responsive than in film or the theater, and the great psychological power of environment is in its conveyance of a sense of continuity and reality. Large spectacles may be disturbing as well as expensive and elephantine. The characteristics of a successful art of this kind will surely be simplicity, rhythm, slow pace, grandeur, an emphasis on the enduring background, a direct connection with natural changes and environmental meaning, a strong reference to human activity.

Design for Motion

It is possible to achieve similar dynamic impressions by using the motion of the observer: the environment appears to change as he traverses it. Once again, since the change occurs in the experienced present, most of the techniques of the temporal arts are available to the designer, at least in a crude form. The long formal approaches to thrones and altars built by kings and priests to awe the suppliant are classic examples. They are simple rhythmic progressions, however rich and massive the materials employed, building to a final climax of splendor or dread, designed to read in one direction under controlled conditions. Gardens and cities have similar processional ways.

In some large gardens another kind of sequence has been designed: a series of contrasting settings meant to be traversed in such a way that the order in which they are seen adds to the pleasure of the experience. The gardens at Stourhead, to take one example, are designed as a delightful circuit about a created lake of irregular form, in which one view follows another, opening and closing among varying plantings, seen from low or high, aimed at structures of successively diverse character and association.

Our lives are full of the delights and the displeasures of motion: highways, city streets, and country walks are often dull but sometimes, quite by accident, joyous or amazing. Spaces seem to change, views open up, objects dance and shift; we saunter, skim, or turn. This is an experience to which people readily respond. The great cities are famous for their walks. Scenic drives are widely appreciated. Our new mobility and our new attitudes toward time and change have substantially increased the potential of sequence design. It may be asserted that the moving view is the primary way in which we experience our environment today. Yet sequence design is practiced rarely, and then only in the simplest way. Few of its inherent possibilities for artistic expression have yet been exploited.

The elements and techniques of the art have recently been discussed in the literature, and some attempts have been made to apply these ideas, at least as proposals. The art has particular characteristics that arise from its dynamic nature, its scale, the degree of control, the way in which it is experienced, and the nature of the things seen. It would be tedious to repeat that analysis here. The esthetic effect on the moving observer is similar to that produced by a changing world and can satisfy a sensitivity to dynamic process. The flow of present time

References 26, 104

185

becomes vivid and dramatic. Moreover, the art is directly linked to the basic function of transportation and therefore need not be an isolated esthetic feature, as the direct display of change is likely to be.

Sequence design can be allied to other temporal effects. A road may expose the historical layers of a city—baroque squares in contrast to new shopping centers, ancient foundations at the skyscraper's root. Paths can link places of contrasting episodic quality, as in the stroll garden. On more formal occasions, as on an educational trip, the journey in space may deliberately symbolize a journey in time. Direct changes of light and sound may be used to enrich the apparent changes caused by the observer's motion. But here we skirt the rim of chaos. The rhythmic modification of some scene through which people were also moving would have to be done with strict control. The changes, or the motion, or both must necessarily be simple and direct.

The Patterning of Long-Range Change

There is yet another imaginable mode for the appreciation of environmental change. It would already be a commonplace if we were able to sense the process of change over longer time spans than hours or days. We might then comprehend the months-long process of erecting a building in the same way that we now comprehend the dynamic form of a dance or a film. Clearly, we do comprehend the building process in one sense. We know it is occurring and can time it and predict it. We design it so that it will be efficient. We may also enjoy particular episodes in it, the erection of the steel skeleton or the act of setting the belfry. But it would indeed be a sophisticated observer who would be conscious of the shape of the construction process as an esthetic form or who would have noneconomic preferences for one course of happenings as against another.

Since large environments change continually and do not have a finished form, it would be very apt if they *were* sensed in this way. We could then design long-range change as an art, planning delays, accelerations, and reversals with an eye to their sequential form as well as to their immediate appearance or their economic and social consequences. We might thereby gain a more profound understanding of the meaning of change. Historians, planners, statesmen, economists, or others dealing professionally with long-range change and supported by various devices for exhibiting that change in symbolic compression may have an esthetic perception of the long process. They may enjoy the ebb and flow of nations or the way in which a city grows and restructures itself. But few of the rest of us can stretch our perceptions to that extent. Confronted with processes over a few hours long, we break them into stationary episodes connected by brief or ignored transitions. And so we are back to the episodic designs of our previous discussion. In that sense, of course, a long-range change should be designed to exhibit, at intervals, characteristic and contrasting appearances, while recalling and prophesying past and future stages. It should also be shaped so that its main course is legible. But legibility is a simple intellectual demand rather than a complex esthetic one.

Our perceptual apparatus is limited. We cannot "see" the development of a flower or even of a bamboo, which may grow sixteen inches a day. We are not aware of those rapid movements visible, say, to a fighting fish, whose perceptual units are as short as one-fiftieth of a second. How ill-equipped we are to observe this moving, changing world! Our range of detection is so narrow that we are nearly blind and must use ingenuity to extend our sight. A plant appears unconscious to us, but if we visually speed up its movements by time-lapse photography, the plant seems to become a perceiving, reacting animal. Edward Steichen is currently filming the changes of a rosebush. At the other pole, with still photography and extremely slow movies, Hans Jenney makes Reference 68 visible the rich, strange world of very rapid vibratory motion. In these previously invisible brief shudderings, we now see complex rhythms, elaborate circulations, fantastic growths, violent disturbances.

Is it possible to extend our perceptual reach by artificial means, in order to sense environmental changes that are now beyond that unaided reach? A film compresses twenty-four hours of city changes into three minutes, and a new world is revealed. We take fresh joy in our urban setting; we learn some-

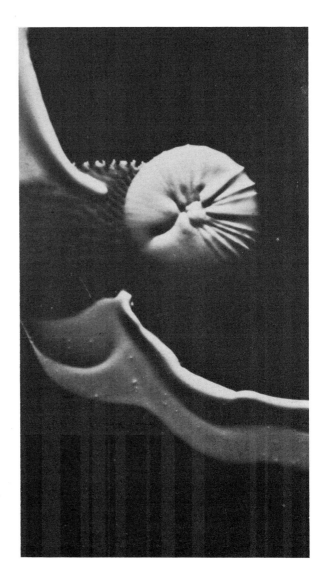

Figure 98
By presenting rapid-
exposure film of a vibrat-
ing, viscous fluid at a
markedly reduced speed,
Hans Jenney lets us see
strange new forms and
motions.

thing about the nature of city processes. Whether we would ever choose to manipulate city form itself in order to produce delightful high-speed or slow-motion changes is problematical. But surely we can envision public devices—films, photos, signs, diagrams—that could bring those invisible processes within everyone's grasp. There might then be "muto- Reference 116 scopes" on the streets, which speed up past and future changes or slow down present vibrations so that we can see them, just as public microscopes and telescopes would extend our perceptual reach.

I have by now outlined four distinct modes in which environmental change can be made into an esthetic experience, and have suggested a fifth and more speculative possibility. By temporal collage, we visibly accumulate the rich traces of past time. By episodic design, we can create contrasting states that resound against our personal memories and expectations and help us organize time into discontinuous, recurrent patterns. By the direct display of environmental change, we dramatize continuous modifications in the present, and by exploiting the observer's motion we gain the same effects even in an unchanging environment. Finally, I have speculated that there are also ways of bringing very rapid or very extended change within our visual grasp and thus within our esthetic experience. All of these ideas open rich possibilities for experiment, for training, and for public participation. While adding directly to our enjoyment of the world, they could also serve to vivify and make coherent our image of time.

8

Managing Transitions

A change in environment may be a growth or a decay, a simple redistribution, an alteration in intensity, an alteration in form. It may be a disturbance followed by a restoration, an adaptation to new forces, a willed change, an uncontrolled one. Changes, when managed, are meant to lead to more desirable states, or at least to avoid worse ones. Nevertheless, all changes exact costs: economic, technical, social, psychological. I shall focus here on the psychological costs: the disorientation, fear, regret, rage, or desolation that change may bring. While doing so, I want to see if there are any special advantages to be pressed out of the various kinds of transition, and how change itself must be conceived of if it is to be managed successfully. I shall assume in doing so that the underlying change is either desirable or inevitable and that the problem is to deal effectively with the transition itself.

Waste and Abandonment

Professionals have been concerned almost wholly with new growth rather than the environment of decline. They do not know how to deal with waste—old farms and scrub growth, derelict mines and buildings, vacant lots, abandoned tenements, accumulated solid waste, old railroad yards, or the space under highways. Some 250,000 acres are derelict in England owing to mining or industrial operations, about one-half of 1 percent of the surface of the nation. In the United States 3.2 million acres are unusable owing to strip mining alone. The solid refuse to be disposed of between 1970 and 1990 is estimated to equal the volume produced from 1900 to date.

Reference 29

If these phenomena are simply regarded with distaste, if our only hope is to hide them or push them farther away from wherever we happen to be, then in time we shall live surrounded by our own excrement. But when we look at waste and scars with interest, we may learn how to integrate them into a continuous cycle of use. Slag is a raw material for cement. Organic waste makes fertilizer. Refuse can be pressed into building blocks or piled into landscape hills, as has been done in Stockholm and is now proposed in Chicago and New York. There

have been major advances in the technologies of
earth moving, soil building, seeding, tree transplan- Reference 84
tation. Flooded gravel pits are good sites for water
sports, other surface depressions for racetracks,
amphitheaters, campgrounds. Old rail and canal
lines can be pleasant pedestrian paths. Old mine
tips may be planted with trees. The citizens of
Stoke-on-Trent have begun to see their industrial
wasteland as a new landscape. The grim, indestructible flak towers of Berlin were covered with the 80
million cubic meters of wartime rubble to make new
hills for recreation in the flat public parks. The
"blacklands" of the English Midlands could be converted into vacation country. Can the empty row
houses of central Baltimore be used as schools, or
playhouses or clubs, or workshops in which to learn
the building trades?

Urban and rural wastelands already serve as a
new wilderness. In lower Swansea, according to John
Barr, "The ruins served as castles and dens, the tips
as bicycle switchbacks. It was a wild and free land
where children could quite literally lose themselves." In Great Britain, there is even an under- Reference 29
current of pride in these scars. "We became black
by determination and hard work. Time-encrusted
grime is part of us in the north of England, and
should stay with us." "People stood it in my day, so
why can't they stand it now?" Purely as form,
stripped of the common associations, a great heap of
rusting automobiles is a wild and impressive landscape. The clay pits of Cornwall are harsh and beautiful.

We do not plead to accept whatever comes. But
if we mean to integrate waste into the cycle of use,
we must modify our automatic squeamishness. We
need to look at it open-eyed, to see its present value so
that it can be exploited for its own unique character.
Since we expect to continue to produce waste, we
must be prepared to reuse, even enjoy, that waste
continuously.

When an entire landscape has "gone to waste,"
we face one of the most painful environmental
changes, and one moreover that we are least prepared to deal with: shrinkage and abandonment. It
is a shift that is borne unequally, as groups are left

behind with obsolete facilities in a broken society. The wasteland creates a disturbing image of death and decay. Yet economic growth and exterior change will often require gradual emigration and progressive abandonment.

Reference 83

And what will our parents do when they grow old? Suppose now that we stayed at home to care for them, maybe we would be threescore years of age before we would lay the last clod on them in Ventry churchyard, and then we would be too old to go anywhere, and who would lay the clod on ourselves?

This species of change is so unpleasant and dispiriting that we neglect it as a technical problem. We shut our eyes to the suffering or try to prevent the change by subsidies and exhortations. But there may be more positive responses to make. For example, it may be possible to move the population as a single group, so that social ties, at least, are not broken and no one is left behind in the midst of decay. A new environment elsewhere may be designed to be similar both in form and in institutions to the old one. Landmarks of memory may be carried out with the emigrants. Prior to moving, they may be instructed about the new area, see movies of its people and places, practice living in simulations of its settings. On arrival, they can be systematically educated to the possibilities of the new location, so that they rapidly become actively engaged in it.

If a mass shift is too difficult or if some people are too attached to the locality to move, there are other strategies. New economic opportunities in the old locale may be sought out. Or communications between old and new places may be so improved that permanent moves are unnecessary and separated individuals can remain in contact with one another and with the familiar location. The old place may become a summer retreat or a symbolic rallying point. Further, it may be possible to concentrate the remaining population and activity in smaller parts of the abandoned locality, clearing and renewing the deserted portions. Local intensity would be maintained; the environmental image would remain clear and free of the pall of decay.

These conditions confront us not only in rural declining regions but also in the inner areas of the

Figure 99
Conical waste heaps in the
pit of a brickmaking area
in Great Britain. When
fresh, their forms have
their own lunar fascina-
tion.

As they erode, collect
water, and are covered
with brush, they come to
seem ancient and gigantic.

great cities. Here the location itself may not be obsolete but may be burdened by obsolete structures and despairing people. Then the problem may be not to evacuate the population but to clear the physical encumbrances and especially to change attitudes toward the future.

Abandonment of the older central areas of North American cities is rising to flood tide. It represents the death of local communities and the loss of low-cost housing. It can be traced to exploiting landlords, to bad tax policies, to unequal services, to public inertia. But it is also the suddenly visible expression of long-hidden shifts outward away from the low-paid jobs, poor housing, and worse services of the center. We look at these empty houses with horror and panic as more and more of them are defaulted to city or federal governments. Might they also be an opportunity for large-scale creative rehabilitation, for urban homesteading, for open space or institutional use, for inner-city new communities? If we run away, we will live in terror of these places.

While it is doubtful that economic development has ever been absolutely blocked by obsolete buildings as distinct from a lack of will or skill or capital or adaptive institutions, certain spatial factors can be important in retarding growth: distribution of the population, basic landform and resources, patterns of land division and tenure, and the network of communications and utilities. Obsolete institutions are more critical retardants, and the attitudes and knowledge of the people who occupy the space are utterly central. Their image of change and the future, their motives, confidence, and ability to accept and organize new information are the prime considerations in producing new growth. Stoke will go to great expense to reclaim its tips not so much because it needs the space thereby released but because it hopes to rebuild confidence and to retain the young people who are leaving.

Environment can teach its users about the nature of change or give them a chance to cause it. The rehabilitation of discarded space, when carried out by the people themselves, can influence their image of change. Analysis of their own condition and of the way it affects them leads people to self-understanding and so to new attitudes and to action. Minor "instant" alterations in the environment can act as a promise, a stimulus, or an expression of impending fundamental change. Things can be wasted and returned to use without being despised. People can also return to new functions without loss of self-respect.

It is a really much easier to cope with external disaster than with abandonment, even though disaster is apparently so much more terrifying. The community may at first be dazed and disorganized, but the aim of planning is clear, some environmental resources remain, and survivors are strongly motivated to rebuild. If the manpower can be rescued, it is almost always possible to restore function. Most areas soon rebound to normal levels, and many develop even further, owing to the new motivations and social mobility that disaster has induced. This is particularly true if basic communications and energy sources are reasonably intact and if predisaster materials standards were high, since there will be surplus resources that can be substituted for the damaged ones. It is rare (and therefore dramatic) to find historical cases of large cities that have been permanently abandoned as the result of a disaster, whereas rapid recoveries are common. Messina flourishes, having survived two shocks of total destruction in this century alone: the 1908 earthquake and the mass bombardment of World War II.

The strategy of any recovery is relatively direct: protect the remaining human resources, reopen the lines of communication and supply, start some visible action quickly, make everyone's image and expectations as clear and secure as possible. Symbolic acts of confidence and orientation are crucial in the early days. London held a royal feast in the ruins, put up the Monument, and spent half its income on St. Paul's and the overbuilt parish churches. The drive to return to the previous situation may be so strong that no modifications in the old pattern can be made, however physically easy and rational. Rebuilding becomes historical reconstruction, the re-creation of the memory image. Exact reconstruction of the Stare Miasto according to old paintings and yellowed drawings made devastated

Disaster

Reference 60

195

Warsaw a *place* once more. The vast rebuilding of the total city could proceed.

Professionals are familiar with conventional growth and have developed systematic ways of dealing with it. An analysis of the linkages between actions allows us to identify those that must come before others or which are likely to be the bottlenecks to prompt completion. Detailed scheduling and monitoring permit quick response to disturbances of the process. We can make a realistic assessment of the rate of change that can be sustained, of the contingencies likely to arise, and of the temporary needs and difficulties that will appear during the transition.

The psychological aspects of transition are less often considered. Processes that may have a desirable conclusion and a well-considered technical order may nevertheless impose frustrating temporary difficulties on the participants and appear to them to be an incomprehensible chaos. The boarded-up buildings of a "renewal" area have become a visual symbol of the futility of public action, and the wrecker's ball has become a new metaphor for evil. Construction can sometimes appear interesting and hopeful; making demolition attractive is not so easy. But smashing things is also delightful, as the crowds at demolition derbies will attest. With a little stage management, the wrecking of buildings could also be turned into a public spectacle, an occasion of awe, of excitement, or of curiosity satisfied by a sight of what's inside. People might leave their memories of a place to be sealed in a memorial at the former entrance, as a reversal of the familiar ceremony for the cornerstone of a new building. Then the rubble must be quickly cleared. Vacant buildings and wasteland should rapidly be put to temporary community or private use, perhaps for the inevitable parking but also for gardens, play lots, exhibits, or clubrooms. Each brief period in the long process of development must be designed to enhance its quality as a time to be lived in.

Reference 115

The nonprofessional is often confused by the visible form of the building process. The pouring of foundations seems to be a hopeless muddle, although

Figure 100
The theater marquee
announces the final drama.

Reference 52

the erection of frame may be beautiful. On one building site, for a few months, confusion may be an insignificant issue. In creating a large environment over many years, however, the perceptual disorder of building—its noise, dust, and inconvenience—can be a more serious affair. Boris Ford, discussing the planning of new universities, notes that the early generations of students will live within an incessant building operation. He concludes that there must be some sense of completeness at every stage of development so that each generation has some visually stable surroundings, some feeling of living in today rather than tomorrow. In any plan, the temporary traffic systems, amenities, and patterns of activity must be as carefully planned as the "ultimate" ones. New kinds of behavior made possible or necessary by the changing environment can be deliberately taught: special signs can explain a new traffic pattern; actors can demonstrate how to use a new plaza. Public chalkboards might communicate not simply the results to be expected in the distant future but the daily operations and targets of the construction process. Observers might begin to see building as a purposeful action interesting in itself, not merely an inexplicable and deplorable inconvenience.

On a larger time scale, changes can be designed to occur in a regular spatial and temporal progression—smoothly outward along a line, for example, or at a growing edge. Signs and symbols of future actions may be placed where they will occur. Thus change is made understandable, the next step can be inferred, and there is no dismaying hiatus. Certain stable centers, streets, landmarks, or topographical forms can be conserved as psychological anchors while the remainder of the environment is being transformed. More difficult, the general pattern may be retained while the specific elements are replaced. For example, an urban center may grow continuously on one side and decay on the other, so that it maintains the same organization and the same gradient of relative age even as it uses up all its parts and constantly moves along in space. Still another policy, one described earlier, is to maintain continuity with the near past, preserving many moderately recent elements and patterns even while losing the more ancient ones. However fast most parts of the environment may change, we are at least in some contact with well-remembered yesterdays. We deal successfully with change only where we can simultaneously preserve some partial continuity—whether of people, things, or places. The very conservatism of the material city may give us the stable frame of reference for some broader social change, as Havana marks the distance traversed in Cuba.

In a more radical sense, we may think of environmental change as a temporal esthetic form, having gradients, sequences, and rhythms that are played out over years of time. We sometimes see such patterns in examining past urban growth, where they result from the operation of organized external forces. Many U.S. cities have clear concentric patterns of housing style as we move out from core to periphery. The way in which the growth of central Boston responded to the location of the original hills and tidal flats is even more intriguing but less obvious. New techniques of change representation make such patterns visible to the professional, at least, and this recognition might be extended to others.

More often than we like to admit, we are not engaged in changing the world to some determined end. We are adapting—responding to outside forces beyond our control, seeking to survive, to preserve something, to maintain some desired level of performance. Although there is a substantial literature on adaptive management in other fields, there is very little that is concerned with the physical environment. We have always focused on newness, growth, and deliberate change.

Adaptation

In managing a large piece of real estate, for example, the market for dwellings fluctuates beyond control, and we renovate, rebuild, change prices or services in order to maintain the stream of income. A municipality administering a central business district is in the same situation, trying to preserve the function and value of the area in the face of uncontrollable fluctuations. In much the same way, people maintain their houses, and institutions maintain their grounds. The role is often masked as being the first step in some long-range strategy that unfortunately is never implemented very far beyond that first stage. After a brief period of drift, the next plan appears.

It has recently been argued that adaptive management is indeed the only possible mode for public planning—that problems are too urgent, objectives too unclear, powers too fragmentary, our intellectual comprehension of change too feeble to allow of anything but a piecemeal response to difficulties as they emerge. If this stand seems to be the usual overcorrective swing of opinion to an opposite and equally untenable pole, it is still evident that adaptation is a much more frequent phenomenon in environmental control than we have been accustomed to admit. We need to learn not only to adapt effectively but to infuse adaptation with purpose and value. If we do not, the slow drift of incremental adjustment may carry us into uncomfortable waters: the income from property decays, the business district becomes massively obsolete, the institutional grounds grow ugly and overcrowded.

In adaptation, the aim is to maintain some level of performance: income, comfort, safety, adequacy, speed, purity, biological health, delight, visual or social character—or whatever. The aim is also likely to include the prevention of irreversible change or of an excessive rate of change. Good management now depends on good information and a quick response. Flexible form and action must be coupled with a clear concept of desired performance, and actual performance must be monitored to see how it varies with respect to that standard. The standard is itself subject to reappraisal and change. But if the response is by its nature slower than the rate of external variation—if recreational behavior changes more rapidly than we can invent and build new settings for it, if the uses for wood shift faster than trees can grow—then responsiveness will be *in*adaptive. It may then be better to make no response at all.

Experimental environments can be used to prepare for or even to warn of impending changes: a subway disaster may be simulated; a large crowd could be brought in to trample over a section of the unspoiled beach that is threatened by development. A manager may try out a mixed-use structure, or a teacher test novel teaching space. Experiments may even seek to speed and extend the evolution of environment and behavior, to learn where some features just now appearing may later lead.

It is always possible that incremental adaptation will not be adequate because external change is too abrupt or the increments are leading into a sink or the necessary changes are too highly interrelated to allow for any piecemeal adjustment. The manager remembers that adaptive managers may sometimes be inadaptive.

Adaptive techniques are hampered by the common attitude that things should last forever and never change and that if they do change it is for the worse. Actions that restore the previous state are therefore regarded as legitimate, even if it is regrettable that they must so repeatedly be undertaken. But acceding to change—accommodating those new people or that new vehicle—appears as a betrayal. Any action other than restoration should be a comprehensively planned jump to a new, more desirable state, which in its turn will last forever. Changing things without knowing where you are going "in the end" is blind and wrong.

Even the games now used to teach new attitudes of management subtly reinforce some of these old conceptions. The game itself is thought of as endless, fixed, purposeless. Actors have purposes, but they cannot change them, nor can they break the rules of the game. They prosper at the expense of others. The game is immoral and cynical, always in motion but always the same. The possibility that adaptation may mean not only personal survival but joint survival and even joint development cannot be admitted. Reference 20

We require a different psychological basis entirely to play the adaptive game (unless we play it in despair). Ideally, we should play not only for survival but for the grace of doing it, the pleasure of new turns in the game, and the sense of streaming in a "good" direction. We may then begin to hear professional gossip about how so-and-so managed so skillfully in a particular situation.

Migrations occur even when environments themselves are not changing radically. Involuntary long-range migrations are the most painful ones, but short movements also mean serious disruption of social ties and accustomed settings for place-bound people. Even in voluntary moves, there are people who are not consulted—children, the elderly, the housewife—and there are unexpected difficulties for those who come willingly. The small children in apartments for married students are aware of how temporary their abode is, and their feelings about the place are strongly influenced by their memories of the past and their expectations for the future. Is there any way in which this sense of the temporary can be taken advantage of, as a basis for adventure and learning?

Shifts that coincide with the family cycle are common in North America today: the establishment of the new family and its frequent early moves, the moves after retirement, the dispersal of the children. Family lines are spread not only over large metropolitan regions but over the entire country. The moves are in some sense voluntary; they may accommodate a shifting family function, may result in income advantages, or may follow geographic preferences. They apparently increase the efficiency of a fluid economy. But the generations no longer nest within each other. Grandparents or cousins are rarely seen; many of us do not know where our ancestors are buried. Telephone calls and flying visits among the closest kin are some compensation, and so is the retention of portable ancestral goods—or antiques, which are substitute ancestral goods. Or the well-to-do may retain some stable family locale, a summer place removed from economic pressures, for example, which can regularly be revisited. Here the generations can congregate and the symbols of family unity (even graves) be kept together.

Recurrent journeys have become characteristic. Vacation trips are commonplace as well as the annual congregations—of scientists at a conference or teen-agers at Fort Lauderdale. In the future even people of modest means may have access to a string of localities among which they move regularly, following employment, preferred climate, or ritual events in what has been the aristocratic and nomadic tradition. These localities may be no more than empty sites on which mobile housing can temporarily be placed, or they may be permanent dwellings owned by shares or leased for special times of the year. Hints of this pattern already appear among younger or more affluent people. Shall we then begin to move our furniture, pets, plants, or other symbolic objects about with us—even our dead—or shall we leave them distributed in the places we move among?

Large numbers of like-minded people now come together at some arbitrary place on short notice to participate in some common event, and local services are swamped. The family may periodically dissolve into age and sex groupings, as it does in the university and the summer camp. High mobility in late adolescence is already widespread.

Temporary, voluntary movements are desirable and enriching. There are obvious advantages in the diversity of settings and relationships, the shifting roles such movements permit, the enjoyment of new climates, the fluidity of mobile manpower. But people must learn how to cope with multiple houses or frequent moves and how to enjoy them. Local residents and visitors must learn to live with each other and how to act in large crowds. Beyond any individual adjustments, the moves require mobile environments and services to meet the surges of demand: hotel ships, tent communities, temporary utilities, deployable police and medical care. A public agency of wide or shifting jurisdiction may be required to cope with these tides.

Robert Coles describes an utterly different kind of migration as he recounts the thoughts and feelings of the children of the migrant farm workers. Homeless and isolated, they move endlessly through a disapproving world that wants their labor and nothing else. One little girl dreams of something different:

It would be the happiest day in the world if one day I woke up and I had a bed, and there was just me and a real nice man, my husband, there; and I could hear my children, and they would all be next door to

Reference 41

us, in another room, all their own; and they would have a bed, each one of them would; and we would just be there, and people would come by and they'd say that's where they live, and that's where they'll always be, and they'll never be moving, no, and they won't have to, because they'll own the house, like the foremen do and the crewmen and everyone else does, except us.

In a humane society, involuntary migration would no longer be necessary, yet we cannot expect total migration to decrease in volume, and voluntary cyclical moves will certainly increase. The shock of both voluntary and involuntary moves may be softened in many ways, most of them similar to the measures used in dealing with abandonment and decay: by increased counseling and other social services; by group relocation; by using roads and telephones to connect the new locale to the old; by moving among the same round of places; by carrying along symbolic objects or a complete home environment; by moving facilities, services, and institutions along with the population; by education to the new. Relocated people may live in "halfway houses," or join temporary organizations for people undergoing similar transitions. The new environment may be made similar to the old one; or some familiar place, where one "knows how to behave," may be inserted into the novel scene. The mover may be given a choice between a new kind of personal setting (an innovative dwelling, for example) or one very like what he left behind. If carried too far, of course, these devices for easing a move may only seal the individual within his accustomed world. He moves from one place only to its twin. Every large airport in the world is alike, and so the flight seems to arrive at its point of departure.

The best environment for human growth is one in which there are both new stimuli and familiar reassurances, the chance to explore and the ability to return. In a mobile age young people, at least, must learn the skills of adaptation: how to acquire new information, how to relate to strangers, how to make choices. But they must have a home and a center somewhere, a secure base from which they can open out.

From general experience, we know something about characteristics that make a change—in our setting or even in ourselves—satisfying or disturbing. Changes in response to our own plans are most acceptable: in our own garden, living room, or self-built house, or as when we learn to play an instrument, speak a new language, or drive a car. If caused by others, changes are more likely to be accepted if they are rapid and legible—that is, if their patterns and consequences are easy to picture and results quickly confirm expectations. A beheading can be preferable to slow poisoning. As another example, a regularly recurring change or a restoration is less disturbing because its result is familiar.

Where conflicting interests are involved, the change may still be acceptable if disagreements are openly aired and adjudicated before the change occurs and there is no obvious injustice: if all groups gain something, or at least none is seriously damaged. Long-drawn-out changes will be more welcome if they come in modest, deferrable increments. We can anticipate and cope with each new increment as it arises, make occasional retreats with dignity, or increase our competence to deal with further change.

These, then, are the changes that are difficult to bear: those imposed without choice or participation; those that are overwhelming, going beyond one's immediate power of accommodation; those that are illegible, their pattern confused or seemingly random; those unequal and unjust; those that are long announced, late in coming, but whose results do not match expectations. All of them are changes that do not fit our way of conceiving or valuing.

Appropriate strategies of change can be derived from these difficulties. Change should be legible and fairly rapid, concentrated in time or space to make a noticeable difference, yet made up of moderate increments that can be deferred without disrupting the entire process. First actions must be successful, however limited. Actions should build in intensity with time, the familiar "bandwagon" technique. Active groups must derive clear benefit from the change. Even better, the benefit should be widely diffused, and many small groups be involved in initiating the action. We should increase the information about the present and the future, raise realizable expectations, and educate to new needs. We may deliberately create imbalance and frustration, in the hope that the subsequent efforts to restore balance will complete the desired change. (But the frustrations should be confined to those who have the power to correct them!)

There are corresponding counterstrategies: delaying actions or piecemeal objections that disrupt the time order, disperse concentration, or reverse the bandwagon effect. An appeal is made for "comprehensiveness," that is, a demand that no new action be taken until all related actions are taken. The principle may be put forward that change must be sweeping and massive or not be undertaken at all. Strong groups may be given a profitable stake in things as they are, or an interest that is threatened by the change may be caused to be widely distributed. False hopes are raised and current results are discredited. The sacred past is appealed to, and anxiety is roused for the future. The flow of information is choked off, the first evidences of change are repressed with excess force, so as to evoke despair. These counterstrategies are attempts to influence the perception of time and change in the minds of the potential actors.

Conceiving of Change

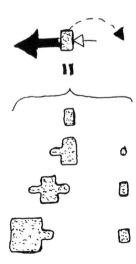

Managing environmental change requires techniques for representing it, or else change would be impossible to plan and control. Present data methods still rely on the assumption that environmental change is a series of stable plateaus interconnected by dimensionless jumps. To overcome this misapprehension, we can use frequent air and ground photographs, continuous field recordings by monitoring devices, periodic spot counts, or dynamic visual presentations to maintain a continuous flow of data on the real, shifting phenomenon. Maps and diagrams should be changeable or must in themselves represent growth and change. Time-lapse movies may be used, or sequential data be stored in the computer, so that we can call up any stage in the process or watch the process in action. By conceptual devices, in other words, we may try to circumvent those very human modes of perception that make dramatic episodes and the ritual passage of time so enjoyable.

Most important of all, we must monitor the user's perception of change: what shifts he is aware of, how he organizes and values them, how he tries to control them.

Both planners and the planned tend to think of environmental change as a troublesome but ephemeral gap between the old and the new, something we can forget after cleaning up the builder's mess. Decision makers are unable to foresee the dynamic effects of development in time or do not wish to foresee them for fear that their strategic "final" aims will be clouded thereby. They may want a modern city, built piece by piece and by hand, without thought that the building and the builders will bring about a very different thing, which will not last forever in any event. They may concentrate on some prime sector, like basic industry, hoping that the changes desired in other sectors will come along by themselves. But industrialization by means of a few basic industries, chosen for their rapidity of effect, may result in an undesirable industrial mix. The pangs of industrialization are judged to be less costly than achieving efficient production, because one is "temporary," and the other "permanent." Yet development is an extended process that must be attended to and valued in itself. It leaves long-lasting traces, both technical and psychological, and no outcome is permanent or final. Is an effect today of less consequence than an effect tomorrow?

The decision maker's perception of change will be reflected in his style of management. He may regard change as a completely controllable process, a problem to be solved, whose terminus is more important than its becoming. The variables with which he deals are few, the total course foreseen, and the objectives fixed. The process itself can be either scheduled in detail or neglected as trivial. In a more sophisticated plan, any uncontrollable disruptions will be forecast and a set of contingency plans prepared that will all converge again to the same desired end.

A similar focus on the final aim, but without such a sense of control, is typical of the military model: hold steadily to a grand objective (strategy), but act today as opportunity indicates (tactics).

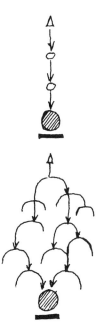

Figure 101
Le Corbusier's housing
development at Pessac in
1926 was acclaimed for its
pure forms, its "func-
tional" design, and its
strong use of unifying
colors. By the 1960s the
inhabitants had modified
these terraces to fit their
own dreams of a comforta-
ble villa.

Alternatively, there may be no final aim other than survival. The manager is a homeostatic device, reacting to exterior change in order to restore equilibrium or the previous state. Or he may be less conservative but equally passive: he lets major events happen and acts to seize whatever opportunity at the moment appears interesting and desirable, enjoying the benefits of chance. Or equally conservative but less passive: he exerts force to keep the world as it is, applying standard solutions and suppressing deviance. Quite in opposition, others desire change itself as an end: the "perpetual revolution."

Each of these attitudes is appropriate when motivation and control fit the model. Determinate environmental planning is reasonable where control is strong and predictions accurate, where the motive is clear and stable, where the planning group is tightly organized, and where the period of change is short enough so that secondary effects are less significant than the final result and the efficiency of getting there. Designing a technical object is a good example. Known means may be employed to reach the desired result, or if there are to be innovations, they will be tested against previously formulated objectives.

Strategic planning is more sensible where control and prediction are poor, the period of change is long, many actors are involved, and efficiency is a relatively unimportant factor. But here the main goal must be fixed, relatively simple, and measurable: to restore the forest, to occupy terrain, to destroy the opposing army, to seize power, to build heavy industry or a city. Only that kind of goal can be communicated and its achievement recognized in the midst of confusion and among many participants. Again, the strategic effort may use traditional means for a traditional end or it may be revolutionary: striving to effect a change that will transform many accepted values and relations and thus in itself bring on unforeseeable subsequent change. A truly revolutionary attitude toward the spatial environment is a dangerous view, although environmental planning will of course be profoundly affected by revolutionary action in other spheres.

The homeostatic model is apt when goals are diverse and conflicting and the situation is poorly understood and difficult to control. The prime actor or regulating agency then has only one simple, constant goal—survival or equilibrium. By the actions he takes to achieve that goal, he resolves conflicts and ensures continuity. Many of his perpetually renewed decisions deal with the allocation of resources among contending parties, others with a defense against sudden threat or the exploitation of some sudden opportunity. In politics the regulator will be a man who wants to stay in office, in economics a market for setting prices.

If such rapid shifts of policy or price are too confusing to permit any forward planning by all the other agents involved, then some partial, recurring, but artificial stabilities may deliberately be introduced: politicians given a guaranteed term of office, prices contracted in advance, the designation of historical landmarks confined to one year in every three. In any case, a constant framework keeps the whole process stable: a consensus on how officeholders are chosen or what honest business practice is. In currency transactions, when fixed parities might break down and lead to apocalyptic jumps, yet unregulated fluctuation raises too many uncertainties for trade, "crawling pegs" are proposed to constrain the rate of change. In a similar way, guaranteeing or limiting the rate of change in environment may be more efficient, both psychologically and economically, than either preservation, on the one hand, or unregulated change, on the other. A maximum, even a minimum, may be set, for example, on the number of dwellings to be built or destroyed in a year. The homeostatic model can operate over long periods and act flexibly as the situation shifts. But the long drift is purposeless and uncontrollable and may degenerate in such a way that all agents lose or the consensus that stabilizes the entire process collapses.

Opportunistic action, which values the process and finds its goals where it can, is appropriate where goals are subtle or unknown, where the communications between participants are sensitive or only one actor is involved, and where the quality of the process is as valuable as that of the product. Control may be strong or weak, but prediction is poor. An artist, a good teacher, or a close-knit group on a holiday works in this manner. The painting seems to grow of itself as the painter adds his brush marks, and his idea of what the painting might be develops as the object changes. A person can build his own dwelling this way or decorate his space. The participant must learn to enjoy the process of change in itself: the constant reformulation of action and aim, the delight of new revelations and new possibilities. The focus is on development and growth and not on a well-formulated end. This is innovative planning again, but now both ends and means are simultaneously and continuously being created. That the attitude is not an impossible one is evidenced by the pleasures of teaching and learning, or of politics, or by the satisfactions of creative design in which form seems to grow like a living thing, enriched by an entire history of past decisions and redirections.

This type of "existentialist" design is now advocated by avant-garde designers for the creation of large environments. But it is a difficult model to apply in situations in which mistakes may be costly and hard to remedy or where communications must be extended and explicit. Its joy is reserved for the participant rather than the passive spectator. It requires rapid and legible feedback of events and of the probable consequences of current action to the participant designers. A painter can explore and develop his forms because they respond rapidly to his gestures, their visual consequences are immediate, and he can judge those consequences quickly by criteria he need not make explicit. To apply this model at a larger scale, there must be more rapid ways of growing and testing environments, whether in reality or as simulations, and users must be drawn into those explorations. Trial environments, manipulable settings, and computer simulations are all possibilities.

The alternate decision model of maintaining the status quo demands powerful control (or weak forces for change), as well as a high valuation on the received state. The objective is clear, but predictions must be accurate and consensus strong. Maintenance is a useful model for the retention of stable

function against the action of well-known, equally stable (usually natural) forces that tend to degrade it. Otherwise, the conditions appropriate to maintenance are found only in some special cases: historic districts or natural landscapes of outstanding quality, where high costs of control may be justifiable. Even there, the model is troublesome, as we have seen. Under the guise of recurrent renewal, however, maintenance may be a way of adjusting to new forces without a conscious admission of that fact.

The model of perpetual revolution locates its values in the process itself—not in its results, but in the states of mind or patterns of social relations that accompany the process. Thus it is as resourceful and flexible as the opportunistic model, yet the goal is relatively simple and communicable among diverse actors. It can sustain revolutionaries through trying times but may be very dangerous where results or subsequent states are important since it can escalate into something totally unforeseen. It is not very clear how it can apply to environmental planning.

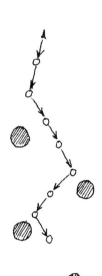

There is another conceivable style that admits and enjoys change, adapts to poor control and prediction and to a fluidity of conditions and objectives but is also active and goal-seeking. Aims are set and actions devised to achieve those aims. As new obstacles and possibilities arise, both aims and actions are revised to meet the changed situation. Unexpected opportunities can be seized upon, the process of becoming is valued in itself, but actions are still directed to an end, albeit a shifting end. Tactics, strategy, aims, and information are continuously revised with experience and, in fact, are not easily distinguishable one from the other. Future obstacles and openings are actively sought out by probes and experiments.

This open-ended style of management is perhaps the one most often appropriate to the dynamics, scale, cost, and long-range implications of large environmental change, where changes are complex, endless, and difficult to foresee. Objectives, constraints, and resources shift and are variously valued by different groups, although basic values may be more coherent and stable. The very process of changing modifies its own conditions at each successive stage.

A builder's camp becomes an integral part of the new city of Brasília; stockpiles of earth destroy valued trees. The new city in Venezuela is constrained by the physical remains and mental attitudes of old plans as much as by its geographical site. Accomplishments can never match original expectations. Past actions and decisions accumulate as "accidental" constraints. There is no completion.

Although it may be peculiarly appropriate, open-ended management is also peculiarly difficult to apply in this case of environmental design, where communications are fragmented, learning is slow, and agents are diverse and numerous. It must be possible to share and analyze early information and tentative goals and actions, to decide on their temporary adoption, and to discard them when necessary. There must be a rapid feedback of results. An expressive common language for conveying problems, possibilities, and criteria is presumed. It must be possible to evaluate the diverse benefits of alternative actions in some explicit way, including a comparison of the benefits of present process against those of future state. But any precision of technique must be sacrificed for a rapid cycling of action and response. Open communications, flexible minds and methods, and an avoidance of fixed hierarchies of status and role are all essential. These are qualities that may, with care, be developed in an expert planning team. We are not yet able to reproduce them in large groups. But current ideas about design criteria and communication, the use of computing machines, participatory research and planning, or the use of nonhierarchical task forces may help. The style is certainly unfamiliar in environmental design today.

Each management style has its niche, and surely there are other styles and other niches. Too often these styles are permanent habits of mind, used inflexibly. If we want to be effective, we shall have to teach various styles of transition management, of which the perception and valuation of time and change are essential parts. Our discussion of the problems and strategies of change has come to focus on this perception and how it can be improved.

We also assert that the nature of visible environmental change can reduce the costs of transformation and help to teach a better concept of change. Shared experience with legible, desired transformation makes people not only used to change but understanding of it. It may even lead them to find delight in it. Environment can be made a symbol and a medium of communication about other kinds of change. The confidence and skill generated by participation in environmental change supports a pragmatic and open attitude.

The very phrase "transition management" connotes a role too limited, too passive, too remote. The world *must* be changed, and environmental transformations can help teach the new attitudes that will make larger changes possible—joyful common action in place of fear.

Environmental Change and Social Change 9

The personal image of change and time has been my subject, and I have discussed how that image affects and is affected by the environment, on the one hand, and the well-being and behavior of the individual, on the other. I have been able to show some connections between the three phenomena: image, environment, and individual well-being. Taking a brief side excursion, I ask in this chapter a question that jumps beyond those connections: If the individual affects and is affected by changes in his environment and if he affects and is affected by changes in his society, what then is the relation between environmental change and social change? It would be satisfying to be able to say that the two changes always occurred together, or that one caused the other, or that they were completely independent. But as one might expect of a relationship working through so many intervening links, the coupling is loose.

Disaster and migration are two cases of rapid and marked environmental change. A stunning environmental disaster may destroy a society or cause it to revert to a more primitive level. This is a social change of a kind, but not a very instructive or desirable kind. More often, a less severe disaster will stimulate a society to make immediate repairs, and in the process of doing so the group will if anything become more rigid and unyielding in its social pattern. Floods, fires, and the physical damage of war have had surprisingly little effect on the course of human social history. A long series of shocks may exert a more telling influence if they sap the basic resources of men and land or call up new social organizations to cope with their continued occurrence: military leadership, for example. But the spatial environment itself is not the key agent of change in this situation.

Changes caused by migration to a new environment are more apparent than those caused by disaster—but not for the nomad, who moves about a familiar territory in a regular cycle, carrying with him his goods and his society and thus changing only a part of his environment and in an unchanging way. Even for the first-generation permanent migrant, for whom a new spatial scene may bring striking release, anguish, or stimulus, that new scene is not very likely to affect his social relationships. Studies of migratory populations point to the astonishing hardihood of social patterns and values. The immersion of individuals or small groups of people in a new social environment will have significant effects, to be sure, and a spatial shift often accompanies that immersion. But we are speaking of the impact of spatial change in itself. Colonies in a new world, with no dominant human societies nearby, tend to be copies of the social systems from which they came and in time reactionary copies. They are likely to modify the new environment to approximate the one they knew or to choose a landscape that is similar to the old. It is the younger people, growing up in the new world, who are more likely to respond to its impact, taking on economic roles that the new environment may permit or demand: hunter, pioneer farmer, city worker. But how American or Soviet the first moon colony will be!

To say this is not to deny the fundamental impact of spatial migration on the well-being of the individual or to forget that there are environmental means of moderating that impact. The spatial mobility often so advantageous for economic reasons has serious human costs, and there are ways of reducing them. Helping people to abandon one living area and to accept a new one is an important task. But I am asking if radical environmental change brings on radical social change. With one general exception, the answer seems to be that in the short run it does not. You do not induce a revolution (although you may cause riots by making people hot when they were cold or by putting them in apartments when they lived in single houses or by dispatching them to the mountains from the plains. Social patterns are persistent. You can affect those patterns by imposing traumatic spatial changes, of course: by closing off all roads, by releasing poison gas, by penning large populations into very small spaces. But these are disasters, and the society upon which they have been imposed will collapse or else reassert itself by reversing your man-made disaster. The social organization built up in the course of that concerted response may be the principal permanent effect of the imposed environmental change.

The general exception to this lack of connection between radical change in environment and society is an obvious one: wherever a feature of environment is directly linked to an important social role, then the modification of the one will cause the modification of the other. The outstanding examples are economic. Enclosure of the common fields in England made it impossible for peasants to act as peasants and forced them into new roles in industrial production. Mechanization of southern agriculture is having the same effect in the United States today.

Where the change in the environment is voluntary, there may be another kind of influence on social organization. If houses or irrigation canals are wanted or there are forests to be cleared or boats to be built and manned, then the new organizations and new leadership called into being to accomplish these aims may have a widespread social impact. Thus an effort to improve housing in the slums using the abilities of the residents themselves will, if it is successful, have some direct effect on their well-being, since they are better sheltered. But it may also have important effects on their attitudes and their organizational skills and thus on their position in society.

Turn the question around: Does social change affect the spatial environment? Perhaps somewhat more, yet also only after a time and often not very profoundly. It is true that alterations in the visible environment can usually be read as a sign of social change: deteriorations or improvements in structures, changes in the use of land, shifts in the visual clues of clothing or furnishings—these are all indexes of social change for the trained observer. But they are often slight clues to which one must learn to attend unless the social change has been concerned with functions directly related to environment: new patterns of land tenure, for example. The city of Havana affords many clues to the profound social changes in Cuban society, but as a spatial organization it is not yet itself profoundly altered. The rural landscape of Cuba is, however, changing in a sweeping way since the spatial form is here directly related to the new organization of production. As another example, the forest landscape in Great Britain has changed markedly but only in response to some specific social events directly connected with it: the growth of the agricultural population, changes in landownership, and the resource demands of war. Important social changes can occur in localities that hardly change at all in a physical sense.

The physical environment is said to be a mirror of culture. It is probably true that in any settled society environment and culture are adjusted to each other. They work together. And we must understand both in order to understand the quality of life. But can we predict the spatial environment from the culture or vice versa? Do similar cultures occupy similar environments? That seems doubtful, except where the relation is tautological, for example, the fact that fishing cultures are located next to bodies of water. Societies often borrow environmental features from one another without necessarily changing their own social patterns.

Should we want to cause a major environmental change, it is usually necessary or expedient to make some selected social changes as well, particularly in the nature of institutions. A new town requires a new form of corporate developer, and the neighborhood commons are maintained by a new homeowners' group. These institutional innovations may in time have secondary effects elsewhere in the social fabric.

We cannot often correlate spatial jumps with social revolutions. When the latter occurs, it is likely to be accompanied by an iconoclasm, a destruction of the symbols of the previous era: crosses, statues, names. Castles are pulled down, towers shortened, monasteries vacated, palaces or temples razed. Even so, the pattern of activity may simply shift within the old spatial container. Although the symbols have been changed, the bulk of the physical setting persists. Too much effort goes into altering the social order to allow any waste of the physical capital previously accumulated. Indeed, most revolutions are under pressure to demonstrate legitimacy, and often they preserve and reuse the old symbolic settings where they can: the new government occupies the palace, the new religion seizes the temple. The environment is used to stabilize an ascendant social order. It might be asserted that revolutionary societies tend to destroy the symbols of the near past and to glorify those of the deep past. They wish to display a radical break with the current order but an attachment to antiquity, to the sacred if inapplicable values. In Cuba, for example, extremely scarce resources are being used to restore the fine Spanish buildings of old Havana and an elegant theater in Matanzas, and these restorations are widely supported.

Any threatened institution, ascendant or descendant, is likely to use environment as a stabilizer: to display its power and its timeless endurance, to reinforce and perpetuate certain ways of behaving. In an age of bank runs, banks were put in solid, classic temples. Kings dealing with dangerous foreign powers receive their emissaries in awesome ceremonial halls. Armies, which must persuade men to go to their death, put them in standard uniforms and sleep them in dormitories arranged with precision.

Environment as Stabilizer

Stabilization is not always a device for manipulation and control. Settings reinforce and perpetuate behavior in a manner that also corresponds to the desires of the behavers: nightclubs are places to be gay and noisy in, studies and churches are for quiet and meditation, beaches encourage us to run and loaf. Environment, like institutions and ritual, helps to transform evanescent actions into predictable repetitions. A shift of the scenery removes that behavioral support, troubling and stimulating the actor. But it may not by itself bring about a change, since many other devices—institution, habit, memory—can be used to perpetuate the old gestures. A coordinated shift of institutions and their settings is likely to be much more effective.

Consciously or unconsciously, the spatial environment has often been used to retard some behavioral change or to throw a cover of continuity over behavior's fluid forms, and so to stabilize our feelings and maintain our emotional orientation. To quote Stuart Hampshire, discussing educational reform at Oxford:

Reference 57

When absent, anyone who thinks of the university thinks first of its essential buildings, and of the extraordinary enveloping beauty, and of the power to dominate, of the scattered colleges and libraries: some of these, in memory, seem to stand for the whole. A great variety of rules of behavior, and of methods of teaching and inquiry, have been and will be fitted onto this setting. Teachers and students might largely re-invent their relations to each other, and the institutions that govern them, without their sense of the identity being lost. . . . While [buildings and their settings] are preserved unspoiled, they will continue to act upon those who are transient members of the university more powerfully than changing institutions do.

We could also speculate about the effects of a very fluid environment, one that responded quickly to shifts in attention and action by its users. Homeostatic places react to change by a counterchange to reestablish the previous state: a thermostatically controlled heating system is the classic example, photoelectric switches on streetlamps are another, and we can imagine extensions of this idea, such as halls that decrease their acoustic reflection as crowd noise swells. But suppose that a room not only adapted to behavioral change but tended to reinforce that change: became brighter and noisier as voices rose, or vice versa; displayed reinforcing visual images of the crowd itself; produced a dance floor and music when dancing began; or exhibited something in more and more interesting detail as more and more attention was paid to it. It might even "learn" to anticipate likely future behavior and to provide the conditions or stimuli for such behavior before it occurred. If the implied technology is expensive, there are simpler examples. We often change the auditory background of a room to suit our mood. The lighting of a public plaza might be programmed to brighten during the course of an important event.

The underlying question, at least, is serious: Could a responsive environment be used to induce behavioral change rather than behavioral stability? If it could, would we want it, except as a toy? Would systems of rapid mutual response between man and setting tend to "blow up," to escalate into uncontrollable action? Limits and dampers would certainly be required. Very likely, an environment of this kind would be too risky and too expensive, except for occasional use under controlled conditions by individuals or very small groups bent on education or entertainment.

In another way, however, environmental change can have a profound effect on the growth and development of individuals and thus, indirectly and at some remove, on the patterns of society. There is substantial, though rather anecdotal, material on the impact of environmental change on the growing child and the adolescent. It is a stimulus to growth if it comes at a time when, with a confidence based on previous stability, he is ready to expand his world. Childhood moves are now common in the United States and seem to be borne reasonably well in most normal families. But if the child experiences those shifts constantly, or too early, or when he is most unsure of himself, he may withdraw and regress. For the adult as well, travel and change, willingly undertaken in an open state of mind, are the occasion for new insights, while imposed change is the signal to cling tightly to old ways, and superficial tourism may cause both visitors and visited to form antagonistic stereotypes.

A setting rich in communication, producing a changing flow of new information, is an education in itself, so long as that information is not overwhelming in its profusion or simply incoherent. Easy access to other settings and other kinds of people, as via a well-developed city transit system, is a good occasion for learning. But those settings must not seem so forbidding or so dangerous that visiting them is discouraged. Safety and a lack of social barriers have as much to do with access as do vehicles and roads. Migration to the great city is the classic occasion for personal development. When our formal schools are in such trouble, it is tempting to look at the educational potential of the environment, where children learn by looking at and acting in real events that interest them.

People learn by doing, and an environment that can easily be manipulated, that invites or that challenges intervention, is an excellent growing medium. The sandbox is a childish example; the family farm has a more extended utility. Thus the

Environment and Learning

Reference 35

environment can be an educational device, an instigator of human change, if it is open and explainable, if it is rich in new information, if it offers the opportunity for the exercise of new functions. A strong potential for "diseducation" is also present in any environmental transition. This loss of learning may be avoided by the careful timing of change, by participation and choice, by the prevention of what seem to be inexplicable, erratic jumps.

Individual development is one of our fundamental values, and we should be willing to devote substantial resources to bring it about. It is also disturbing and occasionally dangerous. A person who has acquired new ideas or skills or habits of mind is a likely agent of further change. Knowing this, conservatives have always paid close attention to the process of education. And revolutionary societies—in Cuba or China, for example—use the environment, by means of posters, broadcasts, and ceremonies, as a vehicle for community reeducation. In our society, learning based upon the spatial environment is more likely to be outside central control. To that extent, a social reformer may be attracted to environment as a lever to use against that center. Unfortunately, the leverage, however powerful, is slow and unpredictable. Moreover, there is always the chance that education may lead to ways of life—dependence on drugs or a strong drive for competitive achievement—that threaten long-term social survival, however pleasant or useful the new ways may seem to be in the short run. Education in an open society needs a balancing and monitoring system, a resistant medium.

I conclude that the relation of environmental and social change is loosely coupled in both directions. Where there is an effect of one upon the other, it is likely to be diffuse—one type of change leading, the other lagging. In many cases, environmental and social patterns tend to act as brakes upon each other. If we seek to cause change in either one, we must understand that partial relationship. We should know what corresponding changes are required in the other sector and whether they will act as triggers, signs, causes, necessary adjuncts, preventives, or dampers. If social or environmental changes are occurring unavoidably, we may use selected changes in one sector to mitigate effects in the other—to smooth out or stabilize a change. Children moving to a new house can be helped to make new friends. Clashes generated by the growth of a new style of life may be softened by spatially isolating the new culture.

It is usually more difficult to arrange a spatial change without unwanted social effects than vice versa, since the spatial environment is the more adaptable of the two, less independent and less self-willed. But the relation of litter and pollution to higher incomes is one example of an unwanted reverse effect operating from society to environment. It is conceivable that cultural evolution has selected for those social patterns that easily survive a physical change, and vice versa. Some degree of uncoupling—forms of society or environment that are adaptable to changes in the other—could have an evolutionary advantage.

Social and environmental changes do not have the same form or the same effects, despite the similarity of name. They both affect the well-being and behavior of the individual, which is our principal criterion of value. Neither social nor environmental patterns are good or bad in themselves, apart from their impact on the human being. They link directly with this central figure through his perceptions and actions, thus only indirectly with each other, and then only in certain limited ways.

10

Some Policies for Changing Things

We try to act rationally for the predictable future and attempt to keep the unpredictable future open and secure. We also want an image of time that is as extended and rich as possible and allows us to live in an active present in harmony with our biological nature. The goals—the psychological objective and the need for future-oriented practical action—are mutually interdependent: we cannot act rationally without that extended and harmonious attitude of mind or think and feel in a satisfying way without being engaged in rational action. These interdependent aims have numerous consequences for environmental policy, and to summarize them is one way to summarize the preceding set of ideas.

The brief tales of cities in Chapter 1 raised many such issues. How can Bath preserve its visual qualities and still function as a living city? How did London reestablish itself after its stunning disaster, and why did the effort seem to fail so soon thereafter and yet succeed in the longer run? How can revolutionary Havana maintain a sense of the past, from which it has so abruptly departed?

How did the London aldermen keep their citizens informed and confident about the future? How can Guayana migrants learn about planners' intentions and so prepare themselves for the changes to come? How can Stoke cope with its obsolete environment and prevent a similar accumulation? Can the renewal and maintenance of Havana be systematized, as the building of new Cuban cities is being systematized? Can Ciudad Guayana be kept an open city both socially and physically?

Could London have addressed itself to its future problems rather than to those of the past? How can the physical city of Havana help to teach the new social aspiration? Can the building of Ciudad Guayana be a means of educating its people? The policies implicit in previous chapters have some bearing on these questions. Let us set them out in an orderly way.

The Organization and Celebration of Time

Public and semipublic agencies should be responsible for structuring and celebrating the passage of time. The environment could be an emblem of

224

the flow of events, communicated in a way calculated to ease our psychological burdens. Most directly, this could be accomplished by the widespread public display of time: time of day, time of season, time of the moon, time of human events. Displays would be not simple clockfaces or bulletin boards but signals whose changing form suited our ways of perceiving. As they made us aware of present and imminent happenings, maintaining our fit to the world outside would become simpler and more natural.

The conventional structure of time, particularly the artificial divisions of hours and weeks, might be examined to see if new divisions are warranted, more closely related to the short and long cycles of the body. Class periods, work shifts, mealtimes should also be investigated from this point of view. Children should be taught to read, follow, and enjoy their own body time. Schedules of work, school, and services might support this aim by allowing more individual variation in timing. Timings are so widely interrelated that any change of this kind may require public initiative.

Reference 10

Many imposed rigidities can be removed. Unnecessary synchronisms can be dissolved. Off-hour services are already increasing as populations to whom they are accessible increase and as older social patterns loosen. Public controls that preserve the old barriers—blue laws, closing hours—are being rescinded. If a sufficient number of people prefer to shop on Sunday or late at night and there are merchants willing to serve them, no obstacle should be interposed. Essential public services—like transportation, food, toilets, medical aid, communications—should be available at any hour, just as fire and police protection are. A premium will have to be paid for this extended access unless social timing becomes much more fluid than it is, since off-hour personal services can no longer be supplied by poorly paid labor working a long day. In densely populated regions the extra cost seems justified and can be shared. Perhaps such services will be an opportunity for teen-age labor and teen-age management. They could become an important contribution from a group that is now largely excluded from the labor market

225

but is the one most willing to shift to new time schedules.

New opportunities for design arise if we turn to the conscious celebration of time. Roads and other channels for movement are already shaped by public agencies but scarcely ever in order to make a trip on them a memorable sequence. We stage occasional public events—firework displays, parades, inaugurations, outdoor concerts and dramas—that do have temporal effects, but they are crudely designed. Few professionals are capable of mounting an outdoor spectacle of light and sound and action in which the audience can join. The responsive environments I have described, on which an observer might play as on an instrument, remain untried. No one makes for us the episodic contrasts we delight in. But there is nothing inevitable about these deficiencies. At relatively small expense we can open up new sources of public enjoyment and expand our experience of being alive in time. Thus our fluid and chaotic urban landscapes may once again seem legible and meaningful.

The skills we need will develop in the doing. New artistic abilities will be evoked, and large technical organizations will come into being. Indeed, we shall have to see to it that the technique does not swallow the art.

Change Intelligence

Providing the essential information about present and future should also be a recognized public function. This includes the visible communication of ongoing change and its probable near-future state, the presentation of alternative and conflicting futures directly connected with present choices of action, the preparation and distribution of forecasts, the creation of a public temporal model of the city, and in general the use of the environment as a device for explaining the advancing present and connecting it with the branching future. There can be automated directories on the streets, public information centers and information playgrounds, tours and guidebooks, films and manipulable models, city guides, street teachers, street theater. Signs and symbols can mark out changes and alternatives on the place itself. Settings of the possible future can be provided for people to try out for themselves. This is public information and education. It is part of a more general concept—to use the city as a gigantic teaching device that systematically exposes children and adults to the rich diversity of people, activities, and forms and encourages them to learn by active involvement.

Some change information is innocuous and welcome to all parties. But information is a source of power, and many future alternatives will be controversial. Their presentation will be subject to political pressure. Operating agencies will try to smother certain disclosures, and advocates for one action will block the communication of opposing alternatives. The information function will have to be protected from censorship, and it must have a built-in motive for success in communication.

Communicating current public intentions and the probable near futures about which there is little dispute can be a straightforward public function. The expression of alternative and conflicting futures and the advocate analysis of current proposals, however, must be divided among a whole range of public and private groups at many levels. There is scope here for private firms and semipublic institutions to make independent analyses of the consequences of some touchy proposal or to produce information that may contradict official data. Without such technical appraisals, small unofficial groups cannot meaningfully debate the future or communicate their hopes and fears to others. Private economic and demographic forecasting enterprises are well established, and so are various product-testing services. But social and environmental forecasting and the analysis of environmental proposals are now largely the work of government agencies or of individuals with insufficient technical support. Advocate testing and forecasting are new and necessary independent functions.

While some of this information may be conveyed by conventional verbal and graphic means and some by dynamic presentations at public information centers, much of it would be more effectively transmitted by symbolic designation on the site itself. It would then become a public responsibility to monitor such transmissions, but only to prevent confusion and mutual interference. Environment as a medium of information has the advantage that there are no serious economic or technical obstacles to decentralization: small groups can speak almost as effectively as large ones. The important step is to develop the means and the clients for an interchange. An important factor in transmitting intelligence of change is a knowledge of how the inhabitants of an area image the past, present, and future. Certainly no environmental alteration should be planned without understanding these common images of time and without considering how alterations will support or enrich them.

Prototypes
Maintaining the flow of current information is not enough. We must actively seek new ways of living in the middle-range future, so that we can judge the desirability of those new ways and keep their approaches clear. This is a new function whose only precedents are the utopian dream or perhaps the technical development of a new commercial product. It will require substantial capital, new skills, and a long-term commitment. Since the payoff is uncertain, distant, and general, exploration of the middle-range future must be partly a public responsibility and partly a responsibility of semipublic institutions, such as universities and foundations.

One possible way of institutionalizing such explorations would be to establish centers to conceive and evaluate possible new environments along with the new institutions and ways of living they imply. When a likely set is developed, it could be tried out at full scale in real time, using volunteer participants, some of whom would be the original designers of the system. Hypotheses to be tested would be part of the design, but the volunteers ("subjects" is an ugly carry-over from psychology) would take control of the experiment once initiated and would progressively modify environment, institutions, mode of life, and hypotheses as partial results accumulated. Thus the investigation would be an ongoing and self-administered study—open, explicit, and recorded but not a controlled test of the classic type. Experiments might be abandoned or sharply modified. If successful, they would be proposed for replication and for communication to others. This is action research, introspective but explicit.

The method cannot disentangle separate causes and effects. Evaluation would have to take account not only of the new environmental features and institutions but also of cumulative historical effects, the external context, the motives of participants, and the microculture that would develop. The prototypes would tend to be apocalyptic since they had not in reality developed out of the present nor would they have had a long period of existence. Nevertheless, how they could grow out of existing circumstances and how they would subsequently flower would be explicit elements of their original design. Furthermore, these assumptions would be explicitly shifted with each change in the course of the experiment. Such a hypothesis for the real-world genesis of a prototype could be tested, perhaps at an accelerated pace, when a successful experiment was being replicated for broader use.

The same centers could diffuse the new possibilities and experimental results to the general public. Individuals might join in as temporary actors, whether for amusement or to help them choose personal or community futures or to train themselves to take up some new life-style. For days, weeks, or months they might play another kind of life. These trials could be particularly attractive to adolescents, vacationers, and decision makers. Or the new prototypes could simply be demonstrated and discussed publicly. Thus people would be encouraged to imagine better ways of doing what they had thought to be unchangeable.

The experimental centers might also be used to test the likely future implications of current or proposed changes in environment and in environment-oriented technology or institutions. By simulation, comparative analysis, or other techniques, the probable system-wide consequences of those changes could be assessed as an aid to public decision making. Comparative studies could also be made of the results of past innovations, intentional or unintentional. The consequences of innovation are rarely analyzed in any systematic way. Techniques of

Figure 102
The demonstration town
in the Summer Palace at
Peking, built to instruct
the emperor about ordi-
nary city life. Palace
attendants played the roles
of shopkeepers, residents,
thieves, officials, and
tradesmen, and the
emperor, strolling down
the main street, could buy
and sell, be accosted, and
otherwise participate in
the street activity, almost
as if he were a private citizen.

monitoring the environment developed in the study of the prototypes could be taught to agencies operating in the "real" environment.

Prototype centers would not be little utopias, nor would they be an escape from society. They would differ from the utopian community of the nineteenth century and from the commune of the twentieth in many ways. They would begin with the real present and show how any new features would grow out of that existing situation. They would not attempt total reform but would experiment by modifying some key variable. Restrictions on the breadth of the change would be imposed both to clarify the results of that change and to make the change easier to achieve by concentrating the innovative effort in one area. The centers would not be isolated experiments. They would be teaching devices, open to scrutiny, designed to return their results to society for testing and replication. They would be realistic, limited, and evolutionary.

At the outset, it might be wise to deal with innovations that were deliberately modest in nature, or even innocuous. In any event, we can think of many possible subjects for trial: environments with new systems of information and communication built into them; environments at unusually high densities; "retarded" or "future-oriented" communities of the kinds discussed in Chapter 3; environments in which new time patterns of activity were being tried out; "responsive" environments or those designed as optimal settings for learning; environments that occupy wastelands or hostile spaces, like undersea, mountaintop, desert, derelict, or high-noise areas; settings designed for small-group control and participation; those built on new ways of raising children or of organizing the family; settlements that are information rich but energy and resource poor, that recycle their wastes and have a high local resource autonomy. The list of possibilities is long. The choice of a strategic beginning would be a nice one.

There are many problems associated with such prototype centers. Not the least is the need to protect the experiments from external disapproval when they threaten existing institutions. Some kind of institutional shield will be needed, and even so, prudence may dictate remote locations for the early ventures and a focus on physical innovations. The experiments would be expensive, and although public or university or foundation support might be obtained in the name of fundamental research, other funds would also be required. The experimental communities might be designed to be largely self-supporting when under way. Fees could also be charged for the information they produce and for the chance to play the future that they offer.

Internal controls would be needed to prevent waste, the alienation of external support, the drift of experiments away from the real problems and possibilities of society, the gradual locking up of key personnel and funds in extended trials, or the possibility of reinforcing feedback that leads to a "blowup" into harmful or fantastic patterns. There is a dichotomy between the enthusiasm and commitment needed in a trial and the flexible, rather impersonal attitude required to design, observe, and analyze these future possibilities.

This is a new kind of research, unlike classical experimentation in its complexity, its mobility of objectives, and its merging of experimenter and subject. In the past, for ethical and economic reasons, we have been limited in our analysis to uncontrolled comparative studies or to impoverished simulations. Prototype design may prove to be a new path to the future; it will certainly be a risky one. The research will arouse fear and resistance. Trials by public agencies will probably have to be confined to less controversial possibilities while more radical proposals are left to independent, semipublic groups. But the risks are small relative to the potential returns, and some such function is essential if we are to keep our future open.

Conservation   Exploring and testing future alternatives can be thought of as one way of maintaining our ability to respond to change. The complementary function of conserving long-term environmental resources and sustaining environmental openness is a crucial public responsibility, and it cannot be lodged elsewhere, although private actions may support it in various ways. The idea of conservation is already an accepted one, but I propose to broaden the term and to disentangle it from the idea of preserving the past.

By conservation I mean not only keeping true basic resources intact (see Chapter 4) but also encouraging the reuse and disposal of environmental waste (derelict space and structure, as well as the more familiar environmental pollutants), maintaining and monitoring adaptability, and keeping a stock of developable space and other environmental reserves. These are expensive actions, but there is political and ethical support for them. Public agencies should be engaged in holding land, purifying streams, and planting forests—these are familiar policies—but also in systematic clearance and acquisition to maintain a land reserve and in the reclamation of derelict urban or rural space.

Public controls must accompany these public actions: to prohibit irreversible damage or to levy the social cost of reversing the consequences of some private act (which might be a high charge, indeed: think of the cost of purifying a city's air, once polluted, or of muting noise, once emitted).

Owners of structures and other improvements might be required to amortize their eventual removal or their reduction to a renewable state as a normal part of the cost of operation. Specific minimum levels of adaptability might be demanded in all new construction. Development rights in land, at least in the critical developing regions, must be publicly owned or periodically acquired by the community. These are costly proposals. Unpaid now, they compound for the future. A strong ethical and emotional basis is required to support such a broad view of conservation.

The wrecking firm and the scrap dealer are private specialists in environmental waste. Their names evoke distaste, yet the functions are important links in the process of development and conservation. The rehabilitation and recycling of wasteland and waste structure must now be systematized and extended. Indeed, we must begin to look on waste, not with repugnance, but as a normal stage in the cycling of material and activity, a stage in itself fascinating and full of potential.

Razing buildings is not the central problem.

The issue is how to return entire complex sites to a productive status or at least to an open and ecologically stable condition that permits future development. Much wasteland, whose use is now blocked by natural defects, fragmented ownerships, old scars, or encumbering engineering works, could be converted to good use. But in planning conversion, we must be aware that "waste" environment may be serving a hidden function—as a "wilderness," for example—and may have unique values not to be discarded lightly.

The most difficult wastelands to convert are those that are also occupied and used, however ineffectively, and where the attachments, interests, and activities of the occupiers are an intimate part of the conditions of the site. Coming to terms with those conditions and allowing the users to join the process of waste removal and rebuilding are things we have not yet learned how to do well. The humane management of waste conversion requires us to deal with the image of change, as well as with many other factors beyond the scope of this book.

We need groups that specialize in environmental clearance and conversion, just as we now have specialists in secondhand books, used furniture and clothes, scrap metal or cars. Such groups would work under public control, with the participation of local occupants. They would necessarily have abilities in community organization as well as in physical clearance. These new organizations could complement or be integrated into firms specializing in large-scale development.

Behind this approach there is an important intellectual task: to develop a theory of environmental disposal. What are adaptability and resilience, how can they be measured, monitored, and achieved? How effective are they in facilitating the response to change? Which kinds of conservation have been useful and which have not? How can environmental waste be reused? Who decides what is waste and what its reuse will be? How can environmental disposal be built into the process of development? To what extent has environmental debris actually impeded social or economic development, and to what extent has it been merely a passing symptom of change? Do decay and waste play any useful role? To the extent that conservation and adaptability have long-range values, how can we compare them to their short-term costs? How can they be internalized as ethical rewards in the present?

Public agencies will be more effective in guiding change than in preventing it. In addition, for reasons previously given, I prefer to emphasize the creation of a sense of local continuity—the tangible presentation of historical context, one or two generations deep, in all our living space—over the saving of special things. That continuity should extend to the near future as well as the near and middle-range past. In any changing area, I propose the retention of some elements, fragments, or symbols of the immediately previous state. Elements least likely to interfere with present function would obviously be chosen, but they should be significant ones, symbolically rich or directly connected with past human behavior or conveying a sense of the total ambience of the past.

There might be incentives for indicating the probable near future or for symbolizing the previous or current presence of individuals and small groups: trees, names, stones, plaques, prints, photographs. Old residents would be encouraged to record their memories of a place. Events of the recent past would be commemorated promptly and very likely only temporarily. Statues and other markers might respond to inquiry with explanatory photographs or recordings about the event or person symbolized. Old ways of doing things would be exhibited alongside their modern counterparts. There could be special areas—"city attics"—in which selected artifacts about to be discarded could be put out for public study and use. And new ways of doing things could also be demonstrated: equipment in a late stage of development and about to be used. Residents and property owners would be stimulated to express their personal intentions and hopes for the near future of the place. The preservation of futures could parallel the preservation of pasts.

The memories and hopes of the users of an area would be the guide for choosing the elements to be retained. The preservation of older structures would otherwise be encouraged only where they had clear present value: characteristics of space, economy, durability, comfort, or esthetic form that could not be duplicated or bettered in new construction. But the present value of older environment would always be analyzed, if for no other reason than to make sure that new construction equaled or bettered those values. Demolition would be preceded by public notice of what was to be destroyed, and therefore there would be an opportunity to record or salvage information from the past.

In special areas of high quality, meaning, or identity, preservation rules could be more stringent, though still not rigid. Consultation on any impending change with specialist advisers and representatives of the local population could be required. The exposure of successive eras of history and the insertion of new material that enhanced the past by allusion and contrast would be encouraged, the aim being to produce a setting more and more densely packed with references to the stream of time rather than a setting that never changed. Only in exceptional circumstances—a Stonehenge, for example—would truly static preservation be attempted (but even the Stonehenge we know today is the accumulated remodelings of a millennium long past). There is a substantial amount of design research to be done to improve our ability to develop such time-packed settings and to guide their progressive enrichment.

In other special areas, public controls might support private or semipublic efforts to develop "outdoor museums": environments in which the entire context of some particular period is preserved and reproduced as accurately as possible, as an educational device. Outdoor folk museums are common in Europe, particularly in Scandinavia (Skansen, Sandvig), and to some extent in this country (Williamsburg, Sturbridge). We could expand this notion by inviting the visitor to play a part himself and thus to acquire a direct feeling for the quality of life in the period represented. By admission fees and charges for lodging, clothing, food, and implements, the museums might defray operating costs or even earn a profit. Furthermore, the subjects would not be limited to the Revolution or the Wild West (although these would be very revealing if accurately done) but would include many more of the critical eras and subcultures of our relevant past, notable and notorious. They should bring people to understand how our society has come to be what it is and what it might now become. They might also explain the life of some isolated group today. This is a troublesome proposal. People will object to some views of the past or to playing difficult roles.

Recent work in industrial archaeology is a good example of the search for a past recent and important enough to have a real connection with our present lives. The remote past is always of intellectual interest and is surely relevant to our understanding of man. But emotionally that relevance is easier to grasp when we have first built a bridge to it across our own time locality.

Reference 63

We might display not only characteristic periods but also the critical transitions, when society shifted in some crucial way—a more difficult objective. It remains to be seen whether physical or social changes can be effectively displayed by compressed-time simulations, for example.

Rather than simply saving things I emphasize the use of saved things to say something. Money gained by forgoing preservation would be spent on education. Preservation rules ought to be simpler and more flexible and yet also more widely applied. In now concentrating our historical anxieties on a few sacred places, where new construction is taboo, we encounter multiple dilemmas: everyday activities progressively decamp, leaving behind a graveyard of artifacts; tourist volume swells, making it impossible to maintain the site "the way it was"; what is saved is so self-contained in time as to be only peculiar or quaint. A sense of the stream of time is more valuable and more poignant and engaging than a formal knowledge of remote periods. New things must be created, and others allowed to be forgotten.

I propose to enlarge the choices among ways of structuring time. Different people would like to feel time passing at different rates; some want to live in the future, some in the past; they prefer to package their days in different ways. For example, I have suggested the creation of areas retarded in technolo-

Time Enclaves

gy—where new devices are prohibited until after long waiting periods have passed and even then admitted only if there is an explicit decision to accept them—where life goes at a slower pace and there are many features remembered from childhood. These areas would make intriguing vacations for some and a welcome refuge from the anxieties and discontinuities of the world for others. The problem would be to ensure that "backwardness" was voluntary for all the residents and to distinguish the essential new technology that must be assimilated. Nostalgic, progress-sheltered communities would answer a real demand and might be profitable for private development.

There are other possibilities of this kind, in addition to the participative museums described earlier. We could arrange special locales, tours, or conventions that would allow time tourists to play new roles in exotic settings or to join in the operation of trial futures. In temporal retreats innovative time schedules might be tried out and programs for teaching new ways of organizing personal time be offered. In still other places of more permanent residence, built for people fascinated by change and the latest inventions, the introduction of new devices might be systematically facilitated.

All these possibilities require substantial capital and managerial skill, since an entire ambience must be created and sustained. But the growing importance of education and leisure and our belated understanding of the plurality of temperament and need together create a market. A nagging difficulty is that the experience so created could be fraudulent: a past with its difficulties removed, a future without commitment. If the deceptive experiences are brief and known to be illusions (Disneyland, for example), there can be no great harm in them. But one would hesitate at more permanent and convincing frauds.

Change Management   Environmental change has been conceived as a single-step jump to a determinate future, in which only one kind of element is in play and transitions have a negligible consequence. The art of change management must, on the contrary, take account of the cumulative effect of transition processes. It must understand the role of timing and strategy, the peculiar linkage between physical and social change, and how physical change can sometimes be used as a lever for accomplishing social change. It must learn to make change legible and acceptable. It must master the technique of "endless" planning, in which goals and situations shift perpetually. It must be able to measure and represent change and to evaluate its cumulative costs and benefits. Public policy must develop instruments that cope with mobility and ease the shock of transition: halfway houses, training for adaptation, the retention of symbolic goods, finding satisfying uses for transitory stages, group relocation, mobile services, and many more.

These are formidable technical problems. Since a just world in which men can fulfill their promise will require great changes, these technical problems are neither socially nor intellectually trivial. Research is needed. But we already have some knowledge about these points, much of it derived from recent experience. To bring this knowledge to bear on environmental management and to create the necessary attitudes are critical actions. We should learn how to accept, cause, and enjoy the continuous process of creation and response—to teach change as well as to manage it.

A new profession may be developing: the manager of an ongoing environment (the spatial and temporal pattern of things and human actions), whose profession it is to help users to change it in ways that fit their purposes. Such a person needs skill in design and in community organization, as well as in the traditional areas of administration and physical maintenance. The roles we are accustomed to —housing manager, maintenance man, caterer, museum director, renewal administrator, planner, architect, community organizer, social worker, developer—do not fill the bill. New skills, new motives, new finances, new rewards, new organizational support must all be created to make such a role possible.

There are difficulties associated with each of the proposals I have made. Some, like prototype research or public celebrations or change management or "time-dense" preservations, require new

Why Not?

239

technical skills. Others—the participative museums, the future settings, the temporal retreats, the spectacles—require the creation of a market and the investment of substantial capital and management skill. Still others—conservation and preservation, special events and round-the-clock services—demand public outlays. But the most substantial obstacles are the political ones—the sectional fears that are kindled and the special interests that are threatened.

Widening time options may generate clashes with ingrained cultural habits of time organization. Radical prototypes will be looked upon with fear. New kinds of preservation will be opposed by those used to looking at history in the classic way. But the fiercest battles are likely to be fought over two other issues. First, a broad conservation policy not only is expensive but runs counter to many private rights in property. Second, a democratic system of public information about future changes and alternatives in environment cuts across the grain of the wishes of many operating agencies and vested interests. These proposals are in two major fields of fire: the issue of private versus public rights in resources, on the one hand, and the struggles between diverse social groups, on the other. My proposals are joined in those larger battles. That they are so connected is perhaps a point in their favor but will not make their accomplishment any easier. Some of my proposals may be carried out with small resistance, while others will generate considerable heat. There will be ways of muting some opposition, as described in more detail earlier, but there are also some fundamental issues that cannot be blinked. That effectuation is worth the cost of overcoming the resistance should by now have been sufficiently argued.

The Image of Space and Time

Effective action and inner well-being depend on a strong image of time: a vivid sense of the present, well connected to future and past, perceptive of change, able to manage and enjoy it. That concept of time must be consonant both with the structure of reality and with the structure of our minds and bodies. I have argued that the form of the environment—the distribution of objects and activities in space and time—can encourage the growth of a strong image of time, can support and enrich it. The argument came out of biological and psychological data on the internal experience of time but also out of literature and art, out of common experience, and out of the problems of real, changing cities. Environmental action can increase our satisfactions today and improve our chances for survival and development tomorrow. But I have not argued that management of the environment is the only way to accomplish those things, nor even that it is usually the most important one.

The concepts of space and time appear and develop together in childhood, and the two ideas have many analogies in their formation and character (as well as some interesting differences). In the logic of science, space and time are now joined. In the realm of art, "space-time" is a fashionable though rather illegible banner. It is clear enough that space and time, however conceived, are the great framework within which we order our experience. We live in time-places.

I have elsewhere discussed the image of the spatial environment—the mental representation of the character and structure of the geographic world—as a scaffold to which we attach meanings and a guide by which we order our movements. This image has an immediate practical role in our lives and a deeper psychological one. "Good" images of place are vivid and engaging, have a firm, resilient, and wide-ranging structure, and allow further exploration and development. Later studies have applied these ideas to settlements throughout the world, and many of the original speculations have been modified by those subsequent studies. The methods for analyzing spatial images, for relating them to the actual behavior of people in space, and for applying knowledge about this relation to the design and modification of real places are now much better understood.

Many parallel statements can be made about the environmental image of time. The same general criteria—vividness and engagement, good structure, aptness for development—seem to apply. The time image is also a mental concept influenced by the form of the environment as well as by other events,

Reference 76

241

and in turn it has an important influence on that environment and on the way people act in it. Both images have intimate connections with the esthetics of landscape, and both have more general but also more loosely linked implications for social structure and social change. It is evident that we should think of an environmental image that is both spatial and temporal, a time-place, just as we must design settings in which the distribution of qualities in both time and space are considered. Places are seen in the mind as changing or apparently static; their character and activity vary rhythmically; they connect with the past and the future. The mental image itself has a history of growth and decay. The psychological dimensions of time and space are not identical—their feel and the data they use are different—but they are linked together. The fit is natural and necessary.

Our earthly environment is a very special and perhaps the unique setting for life. It should be conserved; it cannot be preserved. It will change despite us, whether owing to our intent or to our heedlessness. To the extent that change is inevitable, we should at least make sure that it is a humane process and that it does not lead to our destruction. On the other hand, many needed changes are not inevitable at all. Our real task is not to prevent the world from changing but to cause it to change in a growth-conducive and life-enhancing direction. The environmental image of time-places can play a role in speeding that necessary change, and its analysis can tell us what some of the features of a life-enhancing universe would be. We can change our minds so that we enjoy the dynamics of the world. We can also change the world to correspond more closely to the structure of our minds.

Appendix: Asking Questions

During the investigation of the expression of time in Boston, a group of students was asked to answer an experimental questionnaire. Since some readers may be interested in methods of studying environmental time, this questionnaire and a few comments on it are added here. Some of the data were used in preparing Chapter 6, but for the most part the information is too fragmentary and unreliable to be worth a summary.

The questionnaire itself was only a first trial and has many dubious features. It is uncertain that any written questionnaire is useful for this purpose, since written answers tend to be too abstract and considered, lacking in that dialogue that clarifies a puzzling question or adds depth to a superficial answer. A recorded walk or drive through the city would be better, or perhaps a personal discussion centered on maps, photographs, movies, taped interviews, and other representations of the environment. Nevertheless, the questions given here may be of some interest.

The questionnaire focused on one general location in Boston: the central business district (the CBD). The single focus had the advantage of comparability but also the disadvantage that many interviewees had few ties with that particular place. Among the students were several Boston residents and a larger number of new arrivals, but most of them had been in the city only for a few years, during which time they had visited the CBD just occasionally. Despite frequent puzzlement over the purpose of the questionnaire or the meanings of certain questions, their feelings about the city often burst forth in striking ways. Interesting hints rose to the surface. The questionnaire follows, in italics. Observations on the response to the various questions have been added in brackets.

Please answer all questions, but without taking too much time for thought, even if you know very little about Boston's CBD, and even if a question seems unclear or irrelevant.

1.

In addition to clocks, calendars, and human informants, what clues in the CBD can you use to tell the time of day?
Or to tell the season?
[This question was easily understood, and it produced a rich array of clues.]

2.

On what occasions in the CBD do you find it most difficult to learn when something will happen?
[This one was more puzzling. It was clear, however, that most of these people normally depended on human informants or on nonenvironmental media such as newspapers for temporal information about events.]

3.

On what occasions are you frustrated by being unable to do something in the CBD at some particular time?
[Indeed, they seemed to be frequently frustrated, most often by transportation or by the conventional scheduling of events or services.]

4.

Where in the CBD does time seem to go fastest?
Where slowest?
[Informants understood "fastest," but two different meanings turned up for "slowest." One referred to places that seemed pleasantly calm and leisurely, the other to those situations in which time "drags," as during unpleasant work or impatient waiting.]

5.

On what occasion is the CBD most different from its normal aspect?
What special times of day or season do you like best there?
[Like question 1, this was easily understood and produced much interesting information.]

6.
What part of the CBD is now changing fastest?
What part is changing slowest?
What is the oldest thing in the CBD?
What is the newest thing?
[The question was understood, but it was clear that most respondents were quite poorly informed. They depended heavily on recent, highly visible changes.]

7.
Please enumerate the principal changes now occurring in the CBD that you are aware of.
Which of these is the most significant change, in your opinion?
Which of these changes in the CBD could rather easily be reversed?
Which could probably not be reversed?
[The comment for question 6 can be repeated here. Many of the students expressed a sense of fatality, as though all easily seen changes were irreversible—the product of overwhelming force.]

8.
Which parts of the CBD should be preserved as they are now?
Which should be changed?
[This was understood. There was a remarkable consensus on what should be preserved and a remarkable lack of consensus on what should be changed.]

9.
Which recent changes in the CBD have you found to be confusing or frustrating?
Which changes have you found to be stimulating, or have allowed you to do new things?
What has been the most unexpected change for you?
What changes have had a significant direct impact on your personal life?
[The CBD had relatively little direct personal meaning for this group. The answers to the "unexpected" changes were the most interesting ones.]

10.

Is there anything in the CBD now that reminds you of your parents?
Of your own past?
Of your own future?
Of your children's future?

[Some of the small shops and the bargain basements evoked memories of parents. Nothing seemed to be connected with imagined or desired futures.]

11.

What major changes do you think will probably occur in the CBD in the next twenty years?

[As for questions 6 and 7, they made their predictions primarily by extending present, visible changes.]

12.

If you had to write a history of the CBD and could use only *the evidence you can see in the public environment, what would be the most accurate part of your history?*
The most inaccurate part?

[Most respondents could understand neither the question nor its purpose. They could not imagine themselves engaged in such a peculiar activity. Nevertheless, something like this might be a useful exercise in reality, even if it proves to be a useless interview question.]

For how long have you been acquainted with the CBD, and in what general role (tourist, occasional shopper, employee, explorer, etc.)?
Any comments on the questions?

[My general comments have already been made earlier. Some interesting material came forth—and it would be of further interest to see how different classes of people responded to similar questions. But a dialogue occurring in the presence of the city itself, or among a rich collection of simulations of the city, would be much more evocative. Moreover, it would be better to focus on places of stronger meaning to the respondents: home neighborhood, workplace, vacation ground, or center for essential goods and services. An informal discussion would produce more information, which could be recorded or video-taped to capture more subtle meanings. Respondents might be asked to map the city "as it was," or the changes they expect, or the areas now changing most rapidly. They could be asked about desired changes as well. To understand environmental time as a totality, it would also be necessary to couple any exploration of the temporal image to an investigation of actual temporal behavior. Diaries, questionnaires, and observation would be used to find out what a person actually does at different times of the day or season, where he does it, and whether he has problems of temporal coordination or shortage or surfeit. How a person uses time, how he conceives it, and how those two relate to each other make the complete picture.]

Reference 24

Bibliography

Selected Readings

Page 133

1.
Aaronson, B. S. "Hypnotic Alterations of Space and Time." *International Journal of Parapsychology* 10 (Spring 1968), 5–36.

2.
Bartlett, Frederic C. *Remembering.* Cambridge: Cambridge University Press, 1932.

Page 130

3.
Eliade, Mircea. *The Myth of the Eternal Return,* trans. W. R. Trask. New York: Pantheon, 1954.

Pages 90, 122

4.
Fraisse, Paul. *The Psychology of Time,* trans. J. Leith. New York: Harper & Row, 1963.

5.
Gurvitch, George. *The Spectrum of Social Time.* Paris: Reidel, 1963.

Page 125

6.
Halbwachs, Maurice. *La Mémoire Collective.* Paris: Presses Universitaires de France, 1950.

Pages 121, 123

7.
Hunter, M. L. *Memory.* Baltimore: Penguin, 1964.

8.
Kubler, George. *The Shape of Time.* New Haven: Yale University Press, 1962.

9.
Leach, Edmund. "Time and False Noses." In *Rethinking Anthropology.* London: University of London, Athlone Press, 1961.

Pages 117, 225

10.
Luce, Gay Gaer. *Biological Rhythms in Psychiatry and Medicine.* Program Analysis and Evaluation Branch, National Institute of Mental Health, 1970, Public Health Service Publication #2088.

Page 44

11.
Macaulay, Rose. *The Pleasure of Ruins.* New York: Walker, 1953.

Page 125

12.
Meyerhoff, Hans. *Time in Literature.* Berkeley: University of California Press, 1955.

13.
Miller, G. A., E. Galanter, and K. H. Pribram. *Plans and the Structure of Behavior*. New York: Holt, 1960.

14.   Page 133
Minkowski, Eugene. *Le temps vécu*. Neuchâtel, Switzerland: Delachaux & Niestlé, 1968.

15.   Pages 57, 62
Nabokov, Vladimir. *Speak, Memory*. Baltimore: Penguin, 1969.

16.   Pages 36, 41
Nietzsche, Friedrich. *The Use and Abuse of History*, trans. Adrian Collins. New York: Liberal Arts Press, 1957 (orig. ed. 1873).

17.   Pages 67, 79, 120
Orme, J. E. *Time, Experience, and Behavior*. New York: American Elsevier, 1969.

18.
Piaget, Jean. *The Child's Conception of Time*, trans. A. J. Pomerans. London: Routledge & Kegan Paul, 1969 (orig. ed. 1946).

19.
Shackle, G. L. S. *Decision, Order, and Time in Human Affairs*. Cambridge: Cambridge University Press, 1961.

20.   Page 201
Stark, S. "Temporal and Atemporal Foresight." *Journal of Human Psychology* 2 (1962), 56–74.

21.   Page 116
Toffler, Alvin. *Future Shock*. New York: Random House, 1970.

22.
Whitrow, G. J. *The Natural Philosophy of Time*. New York: Harper & Row, 1963.

23.   Page 131
Yoors, Jan. *The Gypsies*. New York: Simon & Schuster, 1967.

Other References

Page 72

24.
Andersen, J. "Space-Time Budgets and Activity Studies in Urban Geography and Planning." *Environment and Planning 3* (1971), 353–368.

Page 16

25.
Appleyard, Donald. "City Designers and the Pluralistic City." In Lloyd Rodwin and Associates, *Planning Urban Growth and Regional Development.* Cambridge, Mass.: MIT Press, 1969.

Page 185

26.
Appleyard, Donald, John R. Myer, and Kevin Lynch. *The View from the Road.* Cambridge, Mass.: MIT Press, 1964.

27.
Aylward, Graeme. "Environmental Adaptability." MCP thesis, Department of Urban Studies and Planning, M.I.T., 1966.

Page 177

28.
Bachelard, Gaston. *The Poetics of Space*, trans. Maria Jolas. New York: Orion Press, 1964.

Pages 112, 190, 191

29.
Barr, John. *Derelict Britain.* Baltimore: Penguin, 1969.

Page 126

30.
Bohannan, Paul. "Concepts of Time among the Tiv of Nigeria." *Southwest Journal of Anthropology 9* (1953), 251–262.

Page 31

31.
Brandi, Cesare. *Teoria del Restauro.* Rome: Ediz. di storia e letteratura, 1963.

32.
Brandon, S. G. F. *Time and Mankind.* London: Hutchinson Press, 1951.

Page 90

33.
Briggs, Asa. *Victorian Cities.* Baltimore: Penguin, 1968 (orig. 1963).

Page 9

34.
Buchanan, Colin, and Partners. *Bath: A Planning and Transport Study.* London, 1965.

35.   Page 221
Carr, Stephen, and Kevin Lynch. "Where Learning
Happens." In Martin Meyerson, ed., *The Con-
science of the City*. New York: Braziller, 1970.

36.   Page 93
Chi Wu-Fou. "Yuan Yeh," 1634. Quoted in Joseph
Needham, *Science and Civilization in China*, vol. 4,
part 3. Cambridge: Cambridge University Press,
1970.

37.   Page 12
City of Stoke-on-Trent. *Reclamation Programme*.
April 1969.

38.   Pages 87, 163
Clough, Rosa T. *Futurism, the Story of a Modern Art
Movement*. New York: Philosophical Library, 1961.

39.   Page 49
Coggins, Clemency. "Archaeology and the Art
Market." *Science 175*, no. 4019 (January 21, 1972).

40.
Cohen, John. "Psychological Time." *Scientific American*, November 1964, 116–122.

41.   Page 203
Coles, Robert. *Uprooted Children: The Early Life of
Migrant Workers*. New York: Harper & Row, 1971.

42.   Page 41
Corkery, Daniel. *The Hidden Ireland*. Dublin: M.
H. Gill and Son, 1967 (orig. 1924).

43.   Page 109
Cowan, Peter. "Studies in Growth and Change and
the Aging of Buildings," *Transactions of the Bartlett
Society 1* (1963).

44.   Page 41
Cox, Harvey. "The Restoration of a Sense of Place: A
Theological Reflection on the Visual Environment."
Religious Education, January 11, 1966.

45.   Page 102
Craig, Maurice. *Dublin 1660–1860*. Dublin:
Hodges & Figgis, 1952.

46.   Page 49
Davis, Hester A. "The Crisis in American Archaeology." *Science 175*, no. 4019 (January 21, 1972).

47.
de Nouy, Lecompte. *Biological Time*. London: Methuen, 1936.

Pages 41, 126   48.
Dinesen, Isak. *Out of Africa*. New York: Modern Library, 1952.

49.
Dunne, J. W. *An Experiment with Time*. London: Faber & Faber, 1958, third edition.

Page 42   50.
Ekstein, Rudolf. *Children of Time and Space*. New York: Appleton-Century-Crofts, 1966.

51.
Evans-Pritchard, E. E. "Time and Space." In *The Nuer—a Description of the Modes of Livelihood and Political Institutions of a Nilotic People*, pp. 94–138. Oxford: Clarendon Press, 1940.

Page 198   52.
Ford, Boris. In Michael Brawne, ed., *University Planning and Design*. Architectural Association Paper No. 3.

Pages 124, 132   53.
Forster, E. M. *Howards End*. New York: Random House, 1954 (orig. ed. 1910).

Page 66   54.
Frame, Janet. *Faces in the Water*. New York: Braziller, 1961.

Page 123   55.
García Marquez, Gabriel. *One Hundred Years of Solitude*, trans. Gregory Rabassa. New York: Harper & Row, 1970.

56.
Glacken, Clarence J. *Traces on the Rhodian Shore*. Berkeley: University of California Press, 1967.

Page 220   57.
Hampshire, Stuart. "On the Liveliness of Universities." *The Listener 81*, no. 2096 (May 29, 1969).

58.
Hawley, Amos. "The Temporal Aspects of Ecological Organization." Chapter 15 in his *Human Ecology*. New York: Ronald Press, 1950.

59.   Page 107
Hawthorne, Nathaniel. *The House of the Seven
Gables.* New York: Pocket Books, 1971 (orig. ed.
1851).

60.   Page 195
Hirshleifer, Jack. *Disaster and Recovery.* Santa
Monica: Rand, #RM 3079 PR, 1963.

61.   Page 30
Hosmer, Charles B., Jr. *The Presence of the Past: A
History of the Preservation Movement in the
United States before Williamsburg.* New York:
Putnam, 1965.

62.
Hubert, Henri. "Etude sommaire de la repré-
sentation du temps dans la religion et la magie."
In H. Hubert and M. Mauss, *Mélanges d'histoire
des religions.* Paris: F. Alcan, 1909.

63.   Pages 42, 237
Hudson, Kenneth. *Industrial Archaeology.* London:
University Paperbacks, 1965.

64.   Page 173
Hussey, Christopher. *English Gardens and Landscapes, 1700–1750.* New York: Funk & Wagnalls,
1967.

65.   Page 25
International Union of Architects, 7th Congress.
*Architecture in Countries in the Process of Develop-
ment—Cuba.* La Habana, September 1963.

66.   Page 120
Janet, Pierre. *L'évolution de la mémoire et de la
notion du temps.* Paris: A. Chahine, ca. 1928.

67.   Page 36
Joyce, James. *Ulysses.* New York: Vintage, 1961.

68.   Page 187
Jenney, Hans. *Cymatics.* Basel: Basilius Press,
1967.

69.   Page 39
Kawabata, Yasunari. *A Thousand Cranes,* trans.
Edward G. Seidensticker. New York: Knopf, 1959.

Page 126   70.
Leach, Edmund. "Primitive Time Reckoning." In Charles Singer, E. J. Holmgard, and A. R. Hall, *A History of Technology*, vol. 1, pp. 110–127. Oxford: Clarendon, 1954.

71.
Levins, Richard. *Evolution in Changing Environments*. Princeton: Princeton University Press, 1968.

72.
Lewis, Wyndham. *Time and Western Man*. Boston: Beacon Press, 1957.

Page 132   73.
Lifton, R. J. "Individual Patterns in Historical Change: Imagery of Japanese Youth." *Comparative Studies in Sociology and History 6*, (1964), 369–383.

Page 37   74.
Lonberg-Holm, K. "Time Zoning as a Preventive of Blighted Areas." *Architectural Record and Guide*, June 1933.

Page 108   75.
Lynch, Kevin. "Environmental Adaptability." *Journal of the American Institute of Planners 24*, no. 1 (1958).

Page 241   76.
Lynch, Kevin. *The Image of the City*. Cambridge, Mass.: MIT Press, 1960.

Page 128   77.
Moore, W. E. *Man, Time, and Society*. New York: Wiley, 1963.

Page 127   78.
Mumford, Lewis. *Technics and Civilization*. New York: Harcourt, Brace, 1934.

Page 87   79.
Neutra, Richard. *Survival Through Design*. New York: Oxford University Press, 1969.

80.
Newcomb. "Geographical Aspects of the Preservation of Visible History in Denmark." *Annals of the American Association of Geographers*, September 1967.

81.   Page 125

Niane, Djibril Tamsir. *Sundiata: An Epic of Old Mali*, trans. G. D. Pickett. London: Longmans, 1965.

82.   Page 126

Nilsson, Martin Persson. *Primitive Time Reckoning*. Lund: C. W. K. Gleerup, 1920.

83.   Pages 80, 192

O'Sullivan, Maurice. *Twenty Years A-Growing*. New York: Viking Press, 1963.

84.   Page 191

Oxenham, R. J. *Reclaiming Derelict Land*. London: Faber & Faber, 1966.

85.

Papageorgiou, Alexander. *Continuity and Change*. Tubingen, 1970.

86.

Poulet, Georges. *Studies in Human Time*, trans. Johns Hopkins Press. Baltimore: Johns Hopkins Press, 1956 (orig. 1950).

87.   Page 105

Raup, H. M. "The View from John Sanderson's Farm: A Perspective for the Use of Land." *Forest History 10*, no. 1 (Yale University, April 1966).

88.   Page 3

Reddaway, T. F. *The Rebuilding of London after the Great Fire*. London: Arnold, 1951.

89.   Page 53

Rosenbloom, Joseph. "Student Pilgrims Work at Survival in Plimoth." *Boston Globe*, January 27, 1972.

90.   Page 122

Saint Augustine. *Confessions*, trans. R. S. Pine-Coffin. Harmondsworth: Penguin, 1961.

91.   Page 103

Schafer, Edward H. "The Conservation of Nature under the Tang Dynasty." *Journal of Economic and Social History of the Orient 5*, part 3 (1962), 279–308.

92.

Schilder, P. "Psychopathology of Time." *Journal of Nervous and Mental Diseases 83* (1936), 530–546.

93.   Page 171

Smithson, Robert. "A Sedimentation of the Mind:

Earth Projects." *Artforum*, September 1968, pp. 45–50.

94.
Sorokin, Pitrim, and Robert K. Merton. "Social Time, a Methodological and Functional Analysis." *American Journal of Sociology 42* (1937), 615–629.

Page 61
95.
Soseki, Natsume. In E. McClellan, ed., *Grass by the Wayside*. Chicago: University of Chicago Press, 1969.

Page 166
96.
Souriau, Etienne. "Time in the Plastic Arts." *Journal of Aesthetics and Art Criticism 7*, no. 4 (1949), 294–307.

Page 112
97.
Statistical Abstract of the United States, 1971. Washington, D.C.: U.S. Bureau of the Census.

Page 166
98.
Stephenson, Ralph, and J. R. Debrix. *The Cinema as Art*. Baltimore: Penguin, 1965.

99.
Strauss, Anselm, ed. *The American City, a Sourcebook of Urban Imagery*. Chicago: Aldine, 1968.

Page 86
100.
Strong, Roy. *Festival Designs by Inigo Jones*. London: Victoria and Albert Museum, 1969.

Page 99
101.
Svenson, Erik. "Differential Perceptual and Behavioral Response to Change in Spatial Form." Ph.D. thesis, Department of Urban Studies and Planning, M.I.T., 1967.

Page 124
102.
Svevo, Italo (pseud. of Ettore Schmitz). "La Morte." In Appollonio, ed., *Corto viaggio sentimentale e altri racconti inediti*. Milan: Mondadori, 1949.

103.
Toulmin, Stephen, and June Goodfield. *The Discovery of Time*. London: Hutchinson, 1965.

Page 185
104.
Tunnard, Christopher, and Boris Pushkarev. *Man-Made America*, part 3. New Haven: Yale University Press, 1963.

105.
Wallace, M., and A. I. Rabin. "Temporal Experience." *Psychological Bulletin 57* (1960), 213–256.

106.   Page 42
Wallis, Aleksander. "The City and Its Symbols." *Polish Sociological Bulletin*, no. 1 (1967), 35–43.

107.   Page 101
Wells, H. G. *Anticipations of the Reaction of Mechanical and Scientific Progress upon Human Life and Thought.* New York: Harper, 1902.

108.   Page 131
Whorf, Benjamin Lee. "An American Indian Model of the Universe." In John B. Carroll, ed., *Language, Thought, and Reality.* Cambridge, Mass.: MIT Press, 1964.

109.   Page 63
Willetts, John. *Art in a City.* London: Methuen, 1967.

110.
Wolfenstein, M. *Disaster: A Psychological Essay.* Chicago: Free Press, 1957.

111.
Wright, Lawrence. *Clockwork Man.* New York: Horizon Press, 1968.

112.   Page 54
Yates, Frances P. "Architecture and the Art of Memory." *Architectural Design 38* (December 1968), 573–578.

113.   Page 171
Yeats, William Butler. "To Be Carved on a Stone at Ballylee." In *Michael Robartes and the Dancer.* Dundrum: Cuala Press, 1921.

114.   Page 39
Banerjee, Tridib. Personal correspondence.

115.   Page 184
Krasin, Karalyn. Informal suggestion.

116.   Pages 43, 189
Southworth, Michael. Informal suggestion.

Note: Numbers in the margin refer to pages in this book on which the title is cited.

Illustration Credits

37-45. Paul Hagan

46. Print Department, Boston Public Library

47. Paul Hagan

48. George M. Cushing

49-66. Paul Hagan

67. Charles Collins

68, 69. Paul Hagan

70. Charles Collins

71-75. Paul Hagan

76. Print Department, Boston Public Library

77. Yanni Pyriotis

78. Paul Hagan

79. Yanni Pyriotis

80, 81. Paul Hagan

82. Print Department, Boston Public Library

83-88. Paul Hagan

89, 90. Collection of Signorine Luce and Elica Balla

91. E. J. Marey, *Le Vol des Oiseaux*, Masson

92. Ashmolean Museum, Oxford

93. Nan Fairbrother, *New Lives, New Landscapes*, Knopf

94. Metropolitan Museum of Art, Rogers Fund, 1941

95. Yoshinobu Ashihara, *Exterior Design in Architecture*, Litton Educational Publishing, by permission of Van Nostrand Reinhold

96. Alinari

97. Collection: Carroll Janis, New York

98. Hans Jenney

99. Bedfordshire County Council, U.K.

100. Roy Berkeley

101. Philippe Boudon, *Lived-In Architecture*, MIT Press

102. Bibliothèque Nationale, Paris

Index

Piazza del Campo, Siena, Italy, *175*
Pitheads, of potteries, 13
Pits, in landscape, 13
Place
  change of, 40
  "coming of age" of, 178
  continuity of, 61
  and development, 98
  distinctiveness of, 84
  "good" images of, 241
  homeostatic, 220
  local, 89
  names, 41
Plague, 9
Planning
  contingency, 110
  "endless," 239
  long-range, 101
  public, 200
  for successive development, 197
Planning controls, 24
Plants, 79
  as time indicators, 70
  varieties of, 43
Plateaus, change as, 206
Playgrounds, information on, 226
Play leaders, 87
Plimoth Plantation, 53. *See also* Museums
Poets, romantic, 128
Pollution, 93, 103, 112, 223
  international controls on, 106;
  prediction of, 98
Pompey, theater of, *46*
Poor, 6
  and city planning, 8
  of London, 9
  rehousing of, 26
"Poor removal," 42
Population, shifts in, 71
Porcelain, 12
Posterity, 102
Potteries, 12
  village, 12
  waste in, 12
"Potteries Thinkbelt," 13
Poussin, 166
Prediction, 95, 102
  accuracy of, 101
  awareness and, 92
  and wish, 90
Prehistory, 52. *See also* Archaeology
Present, 1
  common, 88
  and concept of future, 92, 102
  eternal, 130, 133, 177
  expansion of, 134
  extended, 131, 177

"great," 177
  immersion in, 84
  influence of, 124
  as mental construction, 121
  narrow, 132
  obliterating, 133
  perception of, 124
  psychological, 79, 122
  purposeless, 131
  remote consequences of, 91
  sense of, 83
Present value, 57
Preservation
  criteria for, 30, 42, 50, 60
  doctrine of, 35
  of environment, 29–31, 235
  future, 115
  historical, 37, 61
  maintenance of, 53
  motives for, 53
  organized movements for, 29
  priority rankings for, 32
  public costs of, 240
  purpose of, 36
  rules of, 236, 237
  strict, 35
Price, Cedric, 13
Primitive societies, eternal present of, 130, 177
Privacy, loss of, 82
Production, duration of, 79
Progression, 198
Promises, and future, 98
Property ownership, London, 3
Prototypes, 228, 232
Proust, Marcel, 124
Psychological anchors, 198
Psychosis
  image of time and, 133
  periodic, 118
"Public attic," 43
Public chalk boards, 197
Public controls, 233
Public relations, 99
Public services, availability of, 225. *See also* Services
Pudding Lane, 3
Puerto Ordaz, company village of, 17
Puppets, 184

Quabbin Reservoir, 108

Rabelais, François, 127
Rail lines, in landscape, 12, 13
Railroad, in Boston, *159*
Rate of time, manipulation of, 77
Rate variation, 181
Real estate, managing, 199
Reality, and time, 240
"Real time," 83
Rebuilding, 195

271